Safety and Justice Program

# Evaluation of National Institute of Justice–Funded Geospatial Software Tools

## Technical and Utility Assessments to Improve Tool Development, Dissemination, and Usage

Carolyn Wong, Paul Sorensen, John S. Hollywood

T0308585

The research described in this report was sponsored by the National Institute of Justice and conducted in the Safety and Justice Program within RAND Justice, Infrastructure, and Environment.

This project was supported by Award No. 2010-IJ-CX-K007, awarded by the National Institute of Justice, Office of Justice Programs, U.S. Department of Justice. The opinions, findings, and conclusions or recommendations expressed in this publication are those of the authors and do not necessarily reflect those of the Department of Justice.

Library of Congress Cataloging-in-Publication Data is available for this publication.

ISBN: 978-0-8330-8567-2

The RAND Corporation is a nonprofit institution that helps improve policy and decisionmaking through research and analysis. RAND's publications do not necessarily reflect the opinions of its research clients and sponsors.

**Support RAND**—make a tax-deductible charitable contribution at www.rand.org/giving/contribute.html

**RAND**® is a registered trademark

# Preface

By federal law, the mission of the National Institute of Justice (NIJ) is to "encourage research and development to improve and strengthen law enforcement" (Pub. L. 90-351, 1968, Part D, Section 402). To carry out its mission and accomplish the mandated research, NIJ issues solicitations to develop capabilities that the law enforcement community can use to improve policing. In recent years, NIJ has funded the development of geospatial software tools with this aim. NIJ requested that the Information and Geospatial Technologies Center of Excellence evaluate a selection of recent NIJ-funded geospatial software tools to determine the tools' impact on law enforcement with respect to whether each tool delivers a new or enhanced capability to crime analysis and how the capability is unique or differs from similar capabilities.

This report documents an evaluation of a selected set of geospatial software tools developed with funds provided by NIJ. The report describes the tools included in the evaluation, our evaluation methodology and framework, study findings, and recommendations based on the findings that will help NIJ maximize the benefits that future geospatial tool developments can have for the law enforcement community. NIJ sponsored the research.

This report should be of interest to NIJ personnel associated with NIJ solicitations aimed at carrying out the institute's research and development mission. The tool evaluations will also interest members of the law enforcement community who practice, study, or research topics related to crime analysis.

## The RAND Safety and Justice Program

The research reported here was conducted in the RAND Safety and Justice Program, which addresses all aspects of public safety and the criminal justice system, including violence, policing, corrections, courts and criminal law, substance abuse, occupational safety, and public integrity. Program research is supported by government agencies, foundations, and the private sector.

This program is part of RAND Justice, Infrastructure, and Environment, a division of the RAND Corporation dedicated to improving policy and decisionmaking in a wide range of policy domains, including civil and criminal justice, infrastructure protection and homeland security, transportation and energy policy, and environmental and natural resource policy.

Questions or comments about this report should be sent to the project leader, John Hollywood (John_Hollywood@rand.org). For more information about the program, see http://www.rand.org/safety-justice or contact the director at sj@rand.org.

Inquiries about NIJ projects should be sent to the following contact:

Joel Hunt
Mapping and Analysis for Public Safety (MAPS) Program
Office of Research and Evaluation
National Institute of Justice
202-616-8111
Joel.Hunt@usdoj.gov

# Contents

# Figures and Tables

## Figures

## Tables

# Summary

By federal law, the mission of the National Institute of Justice (NIJ) is to "encourage research and development to improve and strengthen law enforcement" (Pub. L. 90-351, 1968, Part D, Section 402). To carry out its mission and accomplish the mandated research, NIJ issues solicitations to develop capabilities that the law enforcement community can use to improve policing. In recent years, NIJ has funded the development of geospatial software tools with this aim. NIJ requested that the Information and Geospatial Technologies Center of Excellence evaluate a selection of recently NIJ-funded geospatial software tools to determine the tools' impact on law enforcement with respect to whether each tool delivers a new or enhanced capability to crime analysis, how the capability is unique or differs from similar capabilities, and identify strategies for enhancing the benefits of future NIJ investments.

The purpose of this study task is to evaluate a selection of recent NIJ-funded geospatial software development tools, determine the impact of NIJ's investment in these tools, and develop recommendations based on the evaluation findings for NIJ to maximize the benefits that future geospatial software tool developments can have for the law enforcement community. We focused on the extent to which the tools have been developed and implemented as envisioned, rather than conducting a comparative analysis or formal cost/benefit analysis of the tools.

We worked with NIJ to identify the set of geospatial tools to be included in the study task. Working from an initial list of about 20 tools, NIJ eliminated the handheld tools that will be evaluated under a separate task. NIJ also eliminated tools that were customized to a particular environment (e.g., laws of a state were embedded in the software code) in a way that rendered the tool unusable by law enforcement agencies with different environments without recoding. Table S.1 shows the final set of tools considered in the evaluation.

Table S.1
Geospatial Software Tools Included in the Evaluation

| Software Title | Award | Developer |
| --- | --- | --- |
| ArcGIS 10.2 PySAL Tool | 2009-SQ-B9-K101 | ASU |
| CAST | 2009-SQ-B9-K101 | ASU |
| CrimeStat | 2005-IJ-CX-K037 | Ned Levine and Associates |
| Facility Cop | Adapted from School COP | Temple University |
| GeoDaNet | 2009-SQ-B9-K101 | ASU |
| GeoDaSpace | 2009-SQ-B9-K101 | ASU |
| Geographic Profiler | 2005-IJ-CX-K036 2007-DE-BX-K005 2009-SQ-B9-K014 | Towson University |
| Mobile Semi-Automated 3-D | 2007-DE-BX-K010 2009-SQ-B9-K009 | University of North Carolina at Charlotte |
| Near Repeat Calculator | 2006-IJ-CX-K006 | Temple University |
| OpenGeoDa | 2009-SQ-B9-K101 | ASU |
| PySAL | 2009-SQ-B9-K101 | ASU |
| School COP | 1999-LT-VX-K017 | Abt Associates |
| SPIDER | 2007-IJ-CX-K014 | South Carolina Research Authority and Eastern Kentucky University |
| UCS | 2007-IJ-CX-K014 | South Carolina Research Authority and Kent State University |

NOTE: School COP = School Crime Operations Package. UCS = Urban Crime Simulator. SPIDER = Spatial Pattern Analysis for Investigative Decision Making Exploration and Response. PySAL = Python Spatial Analysis Library. ASU = Arizona State University. CAST = Crime Analytics for Space-Time.

## Evaluation Framework

The evaluation framework developed for our assessments is multi-tiered. There are three basic components at the top level: the technical assessment, the operational assessment, and the overall evaluation. The technical assessment provides a technical description of the geospatial software tool and the environment in which it operates. The technical description is the starting point of our evaluation. It feeds into the operational assessment and the overall evaluation. The operational assessment characterizes the current and potential utility of the tool. The operational assessment also feeds into the overall evaluation. The overall evaluation describes the tool's impact on the law enforcement community with respect to whether the tool delivers a new or enhanced capability to crime analysis and how the capability is unique or differs from similar capabilities. The relationship among the three components at the top tier of the framework is depicted in Figure S.1.

**Figure S.1**
**Evaluation Framework**

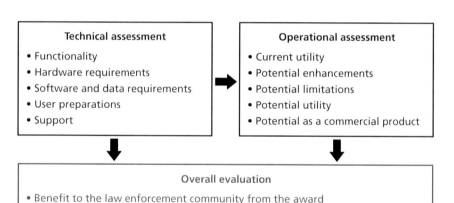

## Evaluation Overview

Twelve of the 14 tool-development awards resulted in fully functional tools for the law enforcement community. In this report, the term *fully functional* means that the tool performs its intended function as evidenced by our independent assessment, user feedback, or developer demonstrations. Table S.2 shows an overview of the evaluation, including brief descriptions of the functionality that each tool is intended to provide, the status of each tool, and any actions needed or being taken to improve the tool.

## Findings and Recommendations

Each of the 12 fully functional tools provided the law enforcement community with a new, expanded, or different capability to address crime. In addition, NIJ selected a spectrum of qualified developers with novel approaches to extend the use of geospatial tools to the law enforcement community. Collectively, the tools provide the law enforcement community with access to new and enhanced geospatial capabilities to improve crime analysis.

For each of the geospatial tools evaluated, NIJ successfully executed the first four phases of the life cycle, from effectively using technology working groups to identify law enforcement needs through formulating solicitations and selecting awardees with creative and theoretically solid approaches to extend the use of spatial analysis to the law enforcement community. The apparent inconsistencies and gaps occur in the phases that follow solicitation.

Our exchanges with developers and users indicate a few areas in which NIJ can take actions to ensure maximal benefits from future geospatial tool developments. These include addressing several apparent policy gaps and inconsistencies, including ensuring that policies assign NIJ or Department of Justice officials roles and responsibilities for the latter phases of software development, including integration and test, implementation, operations and maintenance, and disposition; developing tool-dissemination plans; establishing go-to sources for tool-deployment information; establishing a means to address technical shortfalls in previously funded projects that are now complete; and taking the lead to address emerging interoperability and information sharing concerns.

### Require Delivery of Software Tool as a Condition for Receiving an NIJ Geospatial Software Tool-Development Award

NIJ has not always included a tool-delivery requirement with every geospatial software development award. Although each award must be tailored to the specific development, NIJ should always ensure that the funded tool is delivered to NIJ at some point. We note that NIJ does not always provide all of the funds necessary to develop a functional tool, so delivery of software at the conclusion of NIJ funding might not always be practical. Nonetheless, even in complicated instances, in which multiple funding sources are involved or other unusual circumstances are present, NIJ would ensure that the law enforcement community benefits from the NIJ tool-development award if the institute includes a viable way for it to receive or access a version of the funded product, functional or not, at some point, even if delivery must occur after the delivery of a final report.

### Increase NIJ Oversight During Development so NIJ Is Fully Aware of the Consequences of Major Technical Decisions

Decisions on technical approach can result in unintentionally limiting the potential tool user base. For example, UCS is tethered to Esri ArcGIS Engine 9.2 and reportedly runs only on Windows XP, and neither of these software versions is still in common use. Near Repeat Calculator is incompatible with GPS coordinates. Although resource constraints or the increased complexities of developing a new, unique capability may dictate a particular approach and hence be well justified, full understanding of the consequences by the developer and NIJ before proceeding will still be valuable. For example, in cases in which the developer plans to deviate from platform-independent approaches or existing industry standards, NIJ should encourage the developer to supply justification for the approach prior to tool development. In

**Table S.2**
**Summary View of Observations**

| Geospatial Tool | Function | Action to Improve |
|---|---|---|
| ArcGIS 10.2 PySAL Tool | Tool provides basic spatial regression functionality (spatial lag and spatial error model) and the ability to convert and transform spatial weights matrices within the widely-used ArcGIS | In progress |
| CAST | Allows user to analyze and visualize crimes in space-time frameworks using PySAL functionality | In progress |
| CrimeStat | Spatial statistics program for the analysis of crime-incident locations | Planned release of next version may address user-identified issues. |
| Facility Cop | Prison-incident database creation, mapping, and report generation | Update of School COP can be exploited to update Facility Cop |
| GeoDaNet | Identifies clusters of crimes on networks and calculates distances based on street distance rather than straight-line distance. | In progress |
| GeoDaSpace | Generates views of crimes as function of environmental design characteristics and other variables | In progress |
| Geographic Profiler | Generates probable location of serial offender's anchor point based on locations of offender's previous crimes | Unclear run times can be significantly decreased with software modifications. As computing power of computers increase, prototype run times will decrease. |
| Mobile Semi-Automated 3-D | Provides 3-D location and movement information for first responders | Unclear |

**Table S.2—Continued**

| Geospatial Tool | Function | Action to Improve |
|---|---|---|
| Near Repeat Calculator | Generates estimates of increased probability crime will take place within distance and time of recent crime | Additional investment for GPS-coordinate compatibility and address data input burdens |
| OpenGeoDa | NIJ-funded functionality is spatial data analysis across time | Plan in place, non-NIJ sponsors |
| PySAL | Python-based library of spatial-analysis functions. NIJ-funded algorithms include local cluster detection for polygons, cluster statistics for crimes on streets, computation of street distances between points and crime locations, spatial regression modeling, spatial diagnostic tests for probit models. | In progress |
| School COP | School-incident database creation, mapping, and report generation | Additional investment to update |
| SPIDER | Spatial statistics program for the tactical crime analysis of linked crime-incident locations | Plan in place |
| UCS | Allows users to use their own data to estimate changes in crime rates in their city, at neighborhood level | Additional investment to remove dependence on ArcGIS Engine 9.2 and Windows XP |

NOTE: Shading indicates a tool that was not evaluated because tool was not available or lacked technical maturity to perform an evaluation.

short, NIJ should become a more active participant in all phases of tool development.

## Examine NIJ Policy to Clarify Specification of Roles and Responsibilities to Execute Effective Tool Implementation, Operations, and Maintenance

There appears to be a policy gap at the tool implementation juncture that follows tool development. No NIJ or other U.S. Department of Justice (DOJ) office appears to have taken on the role of tool dissemination and assumed the responsibilities inherent in operations and maintenance of the NIJ-funded geospatial tools. Because many NIJ award recipients are not private companies, they may not have the ability or incentive to conduct such activities with their own funds.

## Create a Means for Developing and Implementing Tool-Dissemination Plans

The utility of geospatial software tools can be enhanced with development of a dissemination plan specific to each tool. Development of a dissemination plan was not included as a requirement for any of the geospatial software developments included in this evaluation. Lack of a basic dissemination plan inhibits the establishment of a tool user base. A basic dissemination plan would identify an appropriate marketing scheme that identifies the potential audience and notifies potential users in the law enforcement community of tool deployment. Such a basic plan would also address operations and maintenance issues, such as establishment of a contact for tool-related questions, error reporting, and suggestions; a tool-update strategy; and tool-retirement criteria. The School COP case illustrates the potential power of dissemination plans. A postdevelopment contract funded by DOJ's Community Oriented Policing Services (COPS) included development and implementation of a dissemination plan for School COP. The result was a large user base that employs School COP on a daily basis to record school incidents.

### Establish and Publicize Go-To Sources for NIJ-Developed Geospatial Software Tools

Our conversations with tool users and developers revealed that there are no established sources (e.g., website, office, publication, app) for the law enforcement community to learn about the existence of geospatial software tools developed with NIJ funding and experiment with the tools. In some cases, potential users were surprised to find that there was an NIJ-funded geospatial tool available free of charge that provided capabilities that law enforcement agencies were buying from commercial sources. Although no comparisons of actual capabilities were made between the NIJ tool and the commercial tools, these comments reveal that some potential users are simply not aware of NIJ-funded tools and do not know where to find out about them.

### Establish Means to Address Technical Shortfalls

In some cases, there are known technical shortfalls with a tool, or user feedback points to modifications that would greatly enhance the utility of a tool and foster closer ties to the operational community. A basic cost/benefit analysis can determine whether a small additional investment by NIJ can mitigate a user issue and make a tool more attractive to potential users. NIJ funding of modifications to address shortfalls in delivered geospatial software tools can result in higher tool adoption and more routine users. Establishing a modest postdelivery modification fund is one possible method of addressing this issue.

### Craft a Proactive Strategy to Address Interoperability as an Emerging Issue for Tool Developers, Users, and Law Enforcement Practitioners

Some of the NIJ-funded tool developments resulted in stand-alone tools that are installed on a single computer and do not have networking capabilities. Others are not interoperable with other tools already in use by a potential user. These characteristics can limit the utility of the tool for a particular user and hence lead to non-adoption of the tool even though the capability may be desired. For example, several users commented that, even though they had the NIJ-funded tools, they did not use them routinely because using them meant that they would have to open another application, prepare the input data files, run the tool, and then try to compare the results with the output from the tools routinely employed. Although none of these steps is difficult, some users view them as burdensome and detrimental to keeping one's train of thought during an active analysis. Ideally, users would have the NIJ tools be extensions that use a single common input database where the user need only specify the data elements to include for a particular tool application and tools could be triggered with a single click. A single common database for a suite of tools is feasible but may require NIJ to take the lead to establish guidelines or standards.

From the developers' perspective, tool adoption is an issue. Law enforcement agencies do not have interoperable systems. Tools often have to be tailored to individual law enforcement agencies. The resource expenditures to effect such tailoring can be costly both in funds and time, and NIJ contracts do not include allowances for adoption.

Information sharing and interoperability of law enforcement information technology are emerging issues that could benefit from NIJ leadership. For example, one agency estimated that making a tool interoperable to share information between two information technology systems required three months to develop, test, and implement transition code after successful negotiation of multiple contracts. The development of national databases, such as the Federal Bureau of Investigation (FBI) facial recognition database will increase the demand for information sharing among national, state, and local law enforcement agencies.

Acting on these recommendations will ensure that NIJ consistently maximizes return on its investment.

# Acknowledgments

We thank Steven Schuetz and Joel Hunt, our study points of contact at the National Institute of Justice, for their guidance and support of this research. In addition, we thank the geospatial tool developers who graciously supplied information on their developments. We also thank the tool users who generously volunteered their time to share information on their tool use experiences. All input received was invaluable in our research. Finally, we would like to extend our appreciation to our colleague, Susan C. Smith, whose postings to the International Association of Crime Analysts discussion membership helped us expand the user base invited to participate in this study. We also gratefully acknowledge the support of Brian A. Jackson, director of RAND Safety and Justice program, and Tom LaTourrette, quality assurance manager for RAND Justice, Infrastructure, and Environment. Finally, we thank the technical reviewers, Jim Mallard, crime analyst for the Winter Park Police Department, and Paul DeLuca and Bradley Wilson at RAND, for their insightful comments.

# Abbreviations

| | |
|---|---|
| 3-D | three-dimensional |
| ASCII | American Standard Code for Information Interchange |
| ASU | Arizona State University |
| bmp | extension for a bitmap file |
| BSD | Berkeley Software Distribution |
| CAD | computer-aided design |
| CAST | Crime Analytics for Space-Time |
| CMU | Carnegie Mellon University |
| COPS | Community Oriented Policing Services |
| csv | extension for a comma-separated-value file |
| dat | extension for a generic data file |
| dbf | extension for a dBASE file |
| DOJ | U.S. Department of Justice |
| dpi | dot per inch |
| FBI | Federal Bureau of Investigation |
| gal | extension for GenePix Array List file |

| | |
|---|---|
| GB | gigabyte |
| GHz | gigahertz |
| GIS | geographic information system |
| GPS | Global Positioning System |
| GUI | graphical user interface |
| html | extension for a hypertext markup language file |
| HTML | hypertext markup language |
| IACA | International Association of Crime Analysts |
| IEC | International Electrotechnical Commission |
| IED | improvised explosive device |
| ISO | International Organization for Standardization |
| JPEG | Joint Photographic Experts Group |
| jpg | extension for a Joint Photographic Experts Group file |
| kml | extension for a Keyhole Markup Language file |
| KML | Keyhole Markup Language |
| LISA | local indicators of spatial association |
| MB | megabyte |
| MHz | megahertz |
| mtx | extension for a Matrix Market file |
| NIJ | National Institute of Justice |
| NYPD | New York City Police Department |
| ODBC | Open Database Connectivity |
| PC | personal computer |

| | |
|---|---|
| ptm | extension for Polynomial Texture Mapping file |
| PTM | Polynomial Texture Mapping |
| PySAL | Python Spatial Analysis Library |
| RAD | rapid application development |
| RAM | random access memory |
| RGB | red/green/blue |
| RMS | record management system |
| School COP | School Crime Operations Package |
| SEI | Software Engineering Institute |
| shp | extension for a shapefile shape file |
| SPIDER | Spatial Pattern Analysis for Investigative Decision Making Exploration and Response |
| SQL | Structured Query Language |
| swm | extension for a split Windows imaging file |
| txt | extension for a text file |
| UCS | Urban Crime Simulator |
| wk1 | extension for a worksheet file |

# CHAPTER ONE

# Introduction

## Background

By federal law, the mission of the National Institute of Justice (NIJ) is to "encourage research and development to improve and strengthen law enforcement" (Pub. L. 90-351, 1968, Part D, Section 402). The purpose of NIJ's research is further specified by law in the Justice System Improvement Act of 1979 (Pub. L. 96-157, 1979, Part B, Section 201):

> improving Federal, State, and local criminal justice systems and related aspects of the civil justice system; preventing and reducing crimes; insuring [sic] citizen access to appropriate dispute-resolution forums; improving efforts to detect, investigate, prosecute, and otherwise combat and prevent white-collar crime and public corruption; and identifying programs of proven effectiveness, programs having a record of proven success, or programs which offer a high probability of improving the functioning of the criminal justice system. (Section 201)

To carry out its mission and accomplish the mandated research, NIJ issues solicitations to develop capabilities that the law enforcement community can use to improve policing. In recent years, NIJ has funded the development of geospatial software tools with this aim. NIJ requested that the Information and Geospatial Technologies Center of Excellence evaluate a selection of recently NIJ-funded geospatial software tools to determine the tools' impact on law enforcement with respect to whether the tool delivers a new or enhanced capability to crime analysis and how the capability is unique or differs from similar capabilities.

## Purpose

The purpose of this study task is to evaluate a selection of recently NIJ-funded geospatial software development tools, determine the impact of NIJ's investment in these tools, and develop recommendations based on the evaluation findings for NIJ to ensure maximal benefit of future geospatial software tool developments for the law enforcement community.

## Approach

We adopted a multipronged approach consisting of evaluations of the selected geospatial software tools for utility and impact. We focused on the extent to which the tools have been developed and implemented as envisioned, rather than conducting a comparative analysis or formal cost/benefit analysis of the tools. The utility assessment consisted of a technical assessment and an operational assessment. The impact evaluation determined the impact the software tools made on law enforcement with respect to whether the tool delivers a new or enhanced capability to crime analysis and how the capability is unique or differs from similar capabilities. Our impact assessments were used to derive the study findings. Recommendations based on those findings focused on actions NIJ can take to ensure maximal benefit of future geospatial tool developments for the law enforcement community.

## Organization

Chapter Two describes our methodology and data-collection procedures. Chapter Three presents our tool assessments. Chapter Four discusses our overall evaluations and the findings and recommendations that stem from the evaluations. The appendix includes descriptions of an international standard and models for the software development life cycle for those who would like further details on the software development process. Finally, the report concludes with a bibliography. The bibliography shows a list of documents that are related to one or more of the geospatial tools assessed in this study or that provide background material on topics related to the use of geospatial tools in law enforcement.

# CHAPTER TWO

# Methodology and Data Collection

## Methodology

The methodology employed for this study consists of six basic steps:

1.  Identify the set of NIJ-funded tools to be included in the geospatial software-evaluation task.
2.  Develop technical and operational assessment frameworks.
3.  Use the assessment frameworks to perform technical and operational assessments of each geospatial software tool.
4.  Synthesize the inputs from the technical and operational assessments to generate a utility evaluation and an impact evaluation for each tool.
5.  Derive findings from a holistic perspective.
6.  Develop recommendations based on findings for NIJ to maximize benefits of future geospatial tool developments for the law enforcement community.

The first three steps of the methodology define the scope of the study, the evaluation framework, and data-collection activity. These elements are detailed in this chapter. Chapter Three presents the tool assessments, and Chapter Four contains the overall evaluations, findings, and recommendations that stem from the findings.

## Tools Evaluated

We worked with NIJ to identify the set of geospatial tools to be included in the study task. Working from an initial list of about 20 tools, NIJ eliminated the handheld tools that will be evaluated under a separate task. NIJ also eliminated tools that were customized to a particular environment (e.g., laws of a state were embedded in the software code) in a way that rendered the tool unusable by law enforcement agencies with different environments without recoding. Table 2.1 shows the final set of tools included in this study.

## Evaluation Framework

The evaluation framework developed for the assessments is multi-tiered. There are three basic components at the top level: the technical assessment, the operational assessment, and the overall evaluation. The technical assessment provides a technical description of the geospatial software tool and the environment in which it operates. The technical description is the starting point of the evaluation, feeding into both the operational assessment and the overall evaluation. The operational assessment, which characterizes the current and potential utility of the tool for the law enforcement community, also feeds into the overall evaluation. Finally, the overall evaluation describes the impact of the tool. The relationship among the three components at the top tier of the framework is depicted in Figure 2.1.

Each of the three components that make up the top tier is broken down to subcomponents. These subcomponents are also shown in Figure 2.1. The rest of this chapter discusses the sub-tiers of the technical assessment, the operational assessment, and the overall evaluation.

### Technical Assessment Framework

The technical assessment component of the framework has five sub-components: the functionality of the geospatial software tool, the hardware required to use the tool, the software and data requirements of the tool, the education and experience needed to use the tool, and

**Table 2.1**
**Geospatial Software Tools Included in the Evaluation**

| Tool | Award | Developer |
|------|-------|-----------|
| ArcGIS 10.2 PySAL Tool | 2009-SQ-B9-K101 | ASU |
| CAST | 2009-SQ-B9-K101 | ASU |
| CrimeStat | 2005-IJ-CX-K037 | Ned Levine and Associates |
| Facility Cop | Adapted from School COP | Temple University |
| GeoDaNet | 2009-SQ-B9-K101 | ASU |
| GeoDaSpace | 2009-SQ-B9-K101 | ASU |
| Geographic Profiler | 2005-IJ-CX-K036<br>2007-DE-BX-K005<br>2009-DQ-B9-K014 | Towson University |
| Mobile Semi-Automated 3-D | 2007-DE-BX-K010<br>2009-SQ-B9-K009 | University of North Carolina at Charlotte |
| Near Repeat Calculator | 2006-IJ-CX-K006 | Temple University |
| OpenGeoDa | 2009-SQ-B9-K101 | ASU |
| PySAL | 2009-SQ-B9-K101 | ASU |
| School COP | 1999-LT-VX-K017 | Abt Associates |
| SPIDER | 2007-IJ-CX-K014 | South Carolina Research Authority and Eastern Kentucky University |
| UCS | 2007-IJ-CX-K014 | South Carolina Research Authority and Kent State University |

NOTE: School COP = School Crime Operations Package. UCS = Urban Crime Simulator. SPIDER = Spatial Pattern Analysis for Investigative Decision Making Exploration and Response. PySAL = Python Spatial Analysis Library. ASU = Arizona State University. CAST = Crime Analytics for Space-Time.

the support material available to the user. These five subcomponents are further broken down into more-specific topic areas. Each topic area includes one or more questions that focus on the intent of the technical assessment input sought for the topic area. For example, one of the topic areas in the software requirement subcomponent is tether-

**Figure 2.1**
**Evaluation Framework**

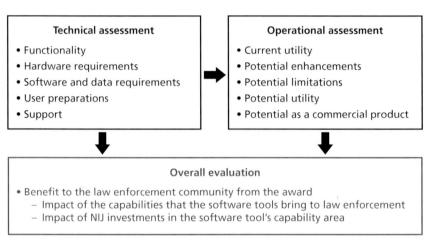

ing.[1] We elaborate on the tethering topic with three inquiries. One inquiry asks for a list of supporting software (licensed software packages) required to use the geospatial software tool. A second inquiry asks about the cost of the tethering software. The third inquiry asks about access restrictions associated with the tethering software.

### Functionality

The functionality subcomponent focuses on what the tool does and includes specific topics relating to tool purpose, verification, responsiveness, validation, output, accreditation, and targeted users. The inquiries associated with the topic areas of the functionality subcomponent seek to discover what the tool does and how well it performs the intended function. The questions associated with each topic area of the functionality subcomponent are shown in Table 2.2.

### Hardware Requirements

For hardware requirements, we tried to focus our inquiries on identifying unusual hardware elements or restrictions that would limit the

---

[1]  Tethered software is supporting software required to run the geospatial tool.

**Table 2.2**
**Technical Assessment: Functionality**

| Aspect | Measure |
|---|---|
| Purpose | What does the tool do? |
| | What does the tool contribute to the law enforcement community? |
| | Is the NIJ-funded version a new capability or automation of a manual capability? |
| | List other tools, if any, that can perform the same function? How well? |
| | Does the NIJ-funded version produce results more quickly than similar products? |
| | Does the NIJ-funded version use fewer resources to provide a useful product? |
| Verification | How accurate is the code and computational processes (e.g., list gaps or "bugs")? |
| | Has the tool been tested against standard data with expected results? |
| Responsiveness | How quickly does the tool respond to user requests (e.g., instantaneous, reasonable, needs improvement)? |
| Validation | Is the fidelity of representation of situational data commensurate with results (i.e., does output change as expected with input)? |
| | Does the tool incorporate the expected information? |
| Output | What information is output? |
| | Is the output displayed in a useful manner? |
| | Is the output displayed in a timely manner? |
| Accreditation | Have users found the output to be useful? |
| Who are the targeted users? | Law enforcement (e.g., NYPD) |
| | Crime labs |
| | U.S. government agencies |
| | International agencies (e.g., English speaking only) |
| | Other |

NOTE: NYPD = New York City Police Department.

utility of the tool. Accordingly, our hardware topics covered the operating system, processing speed, random access memory (RAM), hard drive capacity, video card, display, and support hardware. The questions associated with these topic areas are shown in Table 2.3.

### Software and Data Requirements

The software and data requirement subcomponent seeks information about the software and data required to use the tool along with data formats that are compatible with the tool. This subcomponent covers the topics of tethering software, postprocessing software compatibility, data required to run the tool, data compatibility, input formats, output formats, and registration requirements. Table 2.4 shows the inquiries associated with the software and data topics.

### User Preparations

The user preparation subcomponent is used to describe the education and experience users need for successful use of the tool. The topics for user preparations are what the user needs to know to use the tool and

**Table 2.3**
**Technical Assessment: Hardware Requirements**

| Aspect | Measure |
| --- | --- |
| Operating system | List the operating system required. |
| Processor speed | List the minimum processor speed. |
| RAM | List the minimum RAM to install and run. |
| Hard drive size (available storage) | List the minimum hard drive capacity required to install and run. |
| Graphics board requirement | List requirements. |
| Display | List the minimum dimensions for a usable display. |
| | List the minimum resolution to use the software. |
| | List the minimum number of colors or level of contrast needed. |
| Support hardware | List any required support hardware (e.g., Blu-Ray reader) |

Table 2.4
Technical Assessment: Software and Data Requirements

| Aspect | Measure |
|---|---|
| Tethering | List all required supporting software (other licensed software packages required to use the tool). |
| | What is the cost of the tethering software? |
| | Are there access restrictions to the tethering software? |
| Postprocessing software compatibility | Can the output be exported for further analysis? List compatible software, if any (e.g., ArcGIS, Excel, Access). |
| Minimum data requirements | List any standard or commercial database required to use the tool. |
| Data compatibility | What databases are provided with the tool? |
| | What user-provided data files are compatible with the tool (e.g., census data downloads, user-generated Excel files)? |
| Input formats (free-form or structured) | Is data entry structured or free-form (e.g., city, state, ZIP Code in any order separated by commas, or user selects from predetermined list)? |
| | Does the tool automatically recognize common abbreviations (e.g., *CA*, *Calif*, and *California* are the same place)? |
| Output formats and techniques | List choices of output formats. |
| Registration required | Is registration required to use the tool or data for the tool? |

the number of operators required to use the tool. Table 2.5 shows the questions associated with these topic areas.

### Support

The support subcomponent seeks information about the tool documentation available to users. Table 2.6 shows the questions associated with support.

### Operational Assessment Framework

The operational assessment characterizes the use of the tool. The topic areas of the operational assessment are the current utility of the tool, the potential enhancements and limitations of the tool, the potential

**Table 2.5**
**Technical Assessment: User Preparations**

| Aspect | Measure |
|---|---|
| What does the user need to know to use this tool? | What is the minimum education level (e.g., high school or basic knowledge of policing)? |
| | How many hours of training are required to use the tool? |
| | List the support programs that the user needs to know. |
| Number of operators | What is the minimum number of operators required to use the tool? |

**Table 2.6**
**Technical Assessment: Support**

| Aspect | Measure |
|---|---|
| Documentation | Is there documentation for the NIJ-funded version of the tool? |
| | How complete is the documentation for the NIJ-funded version of the tool? |
| | How current is the documentation for the NIJ-funded version of the tool? |

utility of the tool, and the potential of the tool as a commercial product. The focus points of each of the operational assessment topic areas are shown in Table 2.7.

## Overall Evaluation

The overall evaluation describes the tool's impact on the law enforcement community. We ascertain whether the tool provides the law enforcement community with a new or enhanced capability and characterize how the tool is unique. Where possible, we identify commercial packages that offer similar capabilities and offer a summary comparison.

**Table 2.7**
**Operational Assessment**

| Aspect | Measure |
|---|---|
| Current utility | Does the NIJ-funded version have an intuitive input sequence? |
| | Is the NIJ-funded version's output easy and intuitive to understand? |
| | Are error messages phrased to help the user resolve the problem (e.g., "Inputs limited to 1,000 records" helps the user, while "Error" does not indicate how the error might be remedied)? |
| | How frequently are current users offered updates? |
| | How are users notified of updates? |
| Potential enhancements and limitations | Are there any logical functional extensions to the NIJ-funded version to make it more useful? |
| | What are the main fixable drawbacks of the NIJ-funded version? |
| | What are the main nonfixable drawbacks of the NIJ-funded version? |
| | What would be on an operator's wish list for the NIJ-funded version? |
| Potential utility | What lessons does the NIJ-funded version development offer for future developments? |
| | What is the (anticipated) user demand for the NIJ-funded version? |
| | What role, if any, does the NIJ-funded version have in the long term? |
| | Does NIJ-funded version have use outside of law enforcement? |
| Potential as a commercial product | Has the NIJ-funded version of the tool been, is it being, or is it planned to be transformed into a commercial product? |
| | What is the primary functional or technical barrier for the NIJ-funded version to be transformed into a commercial product? |

## Data Collection

We collected information on the tools from several sources. These sources include the tool developers; tool users; tool documentation, literature, and videos; and team members who independently tested the tools. For each tool, we used information collected from at least two different types of sources. This multisource procedure allowed us to confirm information to ensure accuracy and maximize the objectivity of our tool assessments. The tool developers were identified by NIJ and are shown in Table 2.1. Tool developers provided tool information via questionnaires that included the elements shown in Tables 2.2 through 2.7. Follow-up communications with tool developers were conducted via in-person communications, email, and telephone meetings. Tool users were identified by the tool developers, tool literature, and via inquiries posted to the International Association of Crime Analysts (IACA) discussion membership list. Depending on the users' available contact information and preferences, willingness to share tool user experience, and availability, a subset of the identified users provided tool user information via questionnaires based on the elements shown in Tables 2.2 through 2.7, telephone interviews, or both. We were able to obtain user input for four of the 14 tools. This limited set of user input did not allow us to assess potential biases based on this input set. Tool documentation and videos were downloaded from the tool websites. The tool literature consulted was identified through Internet searches and included a RAND survey on geospatial software tools. Table 2.8 shows the manner in which we collected information for each tool.

As shown in Table 2.8, developer input was not available for Facility Cop or SPIDER. We were unable to identify users willing to share user experiences for Facility Cop, UCS, Geographic Profiler, and Mobile Semi-Automated 3-D. PySAL, GeoDaSpace, GeoDaNet, ArcGIS 10.2 PySAL Tool, and OpenGeoDa had been released very recently, so no user experiences were yet available. CAST has not yet been released, so no user experience could be included. Documentation, website, or literature was available for all except Mobile Semi-Automated 3-D. Finally, independent tests of the tools, except two cases, were conducted. UCS requires outdated versions of Microsoft Windows and Esri ArcGIS Engine software, while Mobile Semi-Automated 3-D could not be made available for testing during the time frame of this study.

**Table 2.8**
**Data-Collection Procedures**

| Tool | Assessment Data Source | | | |
| | Developer | Users | Documentation, Website, Literature, Videos | RAND Tool Test |
|---|---|---|---|---|
| ArcGIS 10.2 PySAL Tool | x | a | x | x |
| CAST | x | b | x | x |
| CrimeStat | x | x | x | x |
| Facility Cop | | | x | x |
| GeoDaNet | x | a | x | x |
| GeoDaSpace | x | a | x | x |
| Geographic Profiler | x | c | x | x |
| Mobile Semi-Automated 3-D | x | c | | |
| Near Repeat Calculator | x | x | x | x |
| OpenGeoDa | x | a | x | x |
| PySAL | x | a | x | x |
| School COP | x | x | x | x |
| SPIDER | | x | x | x |
| UCS | x | c | x | |

[a] Recent alpha release.
[b] Not yet released when this study ended.
[c] No known users.

# CHAPTER THREE

# Tool Assessments

The tool assessments that follow reflect the synthesis of all information gathered from the sources shown in Table 2.8 in Chapter Two. The individual tool assessments are presented in this chapter. The technical and operational assessments of each tool are followed by a discussion of each tool's impact. Each individual tool discussion concludes with a recommendation paragraph in which we suggest an approach NIJ can take to improve the tool's attractiveness to the law enforcement community and thereby enlarge the tool's user base. Because NIJ's mission is to "encourage research and development to improve and strengthen law enforcement" (Pub. L. 90-351, 1968, Part D, Section 402), increasing the tool user bases may be a cost-effective approach to derive more benefit from the tool for the law enforcement community. The information included in this chapter is based on data collected in 2012. The status of some tools may have changed since then.

## ArcGIS 10.2 PySAL Tool

### Technical Assessment
#### *Function*
Esri's NIJ-funded ArcGIS 10.2 PySAL Tool includes basic spatial regression functionality, such as spatial lag and spatial error modeling and the ability to convert and transform spatial weight matrices, packaged for inclusion as analysis tools in this tool.

### Software

NIJ funded the spatial weight transformation and conversion and basic spatial regression functionality. These capabilities are in the alpha release stage. They have been included as part of the alpha release of the ArcGIS 10.2 PySAL Tool under an agreement between Esri and ASU. Esri funded integration of NIJ-funded functionality and released the alpha version of the tool. An ArcGIS desktop license is required to use the tool. The ArcGIS software costs $1,500 for a single-user license.[1]

The ArcGIS plug-in tools are written in the Python programming language and are designed to provide user-interface functionality (e.g., dialog boxes to select data files or fill in parameter values) for ArcGIS. The plug-in tools make calls to the PySAL tool (see PySAL evaluation later in this chapter), and PySAL provides the spatial statistics algorithms. PySAL itself relies on version 1.3 or later of NumPy, version 0.7 or later of SciPy, and version 2.5 or later of Python (see PySAL description later in this chapter). To use the ArcGIS 10.2 PySAL Tool, a user loads ArcGIS. This action automatically loads Python. Next, the user loads NumPy and SciPy, available from SourceForge (SourceForge, undated). The third installation step is for the user to load the PySAL tool from the ASU website. Finally, the user downloads the ArcGIS PySAL tools from the ASU website. These tools are configured to be added to the ArcGIS tool collection. During the time frame of this study, we were able to observe demonstrations of the ArcGIS tools on the developer's machines and they appear to run well, but challenges were present to get the tools working properly on our machines. ASU is working to both update and simplify the installation instructions to overcome challenges for those who wish to use the tools prior to the formal (post-alpha) ArcGIS 10.2 PySAL Tool release. The installation issues are expected to be resolved when the NIJ-funded tools are included in the final release.

### Hardware

The ArcGIS 10.2 PySAL Tool runs on Windows XP or higher. A minimum processor speed of 2.2 GHz or higher is needed. At least 2 GB

---

[1]   Source for price for ArcGIS for Desktop is Esri (undated).

of RAM is also required to install and run the software. A hard drive capacity of 2.4 GB is required for the install alone. Graphic board requirements are 24-bit–capable graphics accelerator and OpenGL version 2.0. In addition, the ArcGIS 10.2 PySAL Tool requires a 24-bit color display with 1,024 × 768 recommended or higher resolution at normal size (96 dots per inch [dpi]) and red/green/blue (RGB) color and contrast.

### Data

Input and output files are .shp or spatial weight files in GenePix Array List (.gal), Matrix Market (.mtx), generic data (.dat), .txt, .dbf, split Windows imaging file (.swm), worksheet (.wkl), GeoBUGS, Stata, MATLAB, or ArcGIS formats.

### User Preparation

The user needs to be familiar with ArcGIS. College-level statistics is required to understand the underlying theory and algorithms. To specify meaningful input and interpret the output, crime-analysis experience must be adequate to understand how the statistics can be used in analyzing crime.

### Support

Download information is available at GeoDa Center for Geospatial Analysis and Computation (undated [a]). ASU is working to update and simplify the installation procedure. A video is available. Documentation is being developed and expected to be available for the ArcGIS 10.2 PySAL Tool release.

## Operational Assessment

### Current Utility

The alpha-test version of the ArcGIS 10.2 PySAL Tool was recently released. No user experience was available in the time frame of this study.

### Potential Enhancements and Limitations

The software is in alpha release. The beta and final release versions may contain additional functionality.

### Potential Utility

The ArcGIS 10.2 PySAL Tool is potentially useful to criminologists and researchers in other fields who need basic spatial regression functionality, such as spatial lag and spatial error modeling and the ability to convert and transform spatial weight matrices. The user base for the tool may expand once a final version is released. The $300 Esri ArcGIS desktop license fee may deter some potential users.

### Potential as a Commercial Product

The developer has no plans to turn the ArcGIS 10.2 PySAL Tool into an independent commercial product.

### Impact

The law enforcement community has not yet had a chance to use the ArcGIS 10.2 PySAL Tool. NIJ provided seed funding to make sophisticated spatial statistical algorithms readily available free of charge to those who use ArcGIS and have the statistical expertise to apply these routines.[2]

### Recommendations

The current version of the ArcGIS 10.2 PySAL Tool is the alpha-test version. The beta-test and final versions can be expected in the future without further NIJ action. We recommend that NIJ include the tool in its publicity for NIJ-funded tools because it makes spatial statistical algorithms available to the large ArcGIS user base that includes many in the law enforcement community.

## Crime Analytics for Space-Time

### Technical Assessment

#### Function

CAST allows the user to analyze and visualize crimes in space-time frameworks. Its space-time cluster methods and other spatial-analysis

---

[2]  The ArcGIS 10.2 PySAL Tool is free to those with access to ArcGIS, but access to ArcGIS requires a fee.

tools can be used by law enforcement for detecting patterns in crimes across space and time.

## Software

This evaluation is based on a demonstration of a pre–alpha release version of CAST. CAST is in active development and has not yet been released. Download of the alpha release is anticipated to be available in the near future.

The NIJ-funded functionality in CAST includes time-enabled local cluster detection for polygons, LISA Markov statistic for cluster persistence over time, LISA Markov heat map, trend graph of crimes, crime calendar view and heat map linked to map, scatterplot, boxplot, maps to identify outliers, kernel density maps, and histograms. CAST will allow crime events to be aggregated on the fly to areas. Map views and tables will be linked when observations are selected, and queries will allow for specification of time intervals and crime types.

## Hardware

CAST will run on Windows XP or more-recent versions of Windows, Mac OS X or more-recent Mac operating systems, and Linux. A minimum processor speed of 1.0 GHz is recommended (300 MHz for Windows XP; 1 GHz for Windows 7; 867 MHz for Mac OS X 10.5), but it will run on slower processors. A minimum of 512 MB RAM is recommended to install and run (64 MB for Windows XP; 1 GB for Windows 7; 512 MB for Mac OS X 10.5), but CAST will run on systems with less RAM. A minimum hard drive capacity of 10 GB is recommended to install and run (Windows XP requires 1.5 GB, Windows 7 requires 15 GB, Mac OS X 10.4 requires 3 GB, and Mac OS X 10.5 requires 9 GB). A graphics board that supports DirectX 9 and OpenGL 1.0 is required. Because CAST will display multiple views of crime data (each view in a separate pop-up window), a 13-inch (diagonal) display with a minimum of 800 × 600 resolution and RGB color and contrast is required.

CAST is available at GeoDa Center for Geospatial Analysis and Computation (undated [b]).

*Data*

Input and output files will be .shp.

*User Preparations*

College-level statistics is required to understand the underlying routines. Crime-analysis experience along with college-level statistics is needed to specify the input and interpret the output.

*Support*

The developer is in the process of generating support material.

## Operational Assessment
*Current Utility*

The software tool has not yet been released.

*Potential Enhancements and Limitations*

The software is in active development. The alpha, beta, and final release versions may contain functionality not available in the pre–alpha release demonstration version.

*Potential Utility*

The pre–alpha release demonstration version of CAST is quite impressive. Because no known program offers the capabilities in CAST, crime analysts may find this geospatial software tool a valuable addition to their toolkits.

*Potential as a Commercial Product*

The developer has no plans to turn CAST into a commercial product.

## Impact

The software tool had not yet been released during the time frame of the study. The alpha version is now available at GeoDa Center for Geospatial Analysis and Computation (undated [b]).

## Recommendations

CAST is a tool that allows the user to analyze and visualize crimes in space-time frameworks. CAST documentation is being developed. Once CAST is released, NIJ should include it in its publicity for NIJ-funded tools because it will offer space-time cluster methods and other spatial-analysis tools that can be used by law enforcement for detecting patterns in crimes across space and time.

## CrimeStat

### Technical Assessment
*Function*

CrimeStat is a spatial statistics program for the analysis of crime-incident locations. It can perform a wide range of statistical calculations on geocoded crime data and output a variety of spatial statistics. Among the routines available to the user are spatial description functions, such as statistics for describing the spatial distribution of incidents (e.g., mean center), spatial autocorrelation statistics (e.g., general spatial autocorrelation indices, such as Moran's I and Geary's C), distance-analysis functions (e.g., Ripley's K statistic), and hot spot–analysis functions (e.g., k-means clustering). CrimeStat's spatial modeling functions include interpolation, space-time analysis, journey-to-crime analysis, and regression modeling. Crime travel-demand modeling functions, such as predictions of the number of crimes in each zone, trip distribution, travel modes, and likely trip routes, are also available in CrimeStat.

*Software*

CrimeStat provides supplemental statistical tools to aid law enforcement agencies and criminal justice researchers in their crime-mapping efforts. It reads geocoded files that specify the locations of crimes. The input files can be in dBASE format (.dbf), shapefile shape format (.shp), American Standard Code for Information Interchange (ASCII) format, or Open Database Connectivity (ODBC)–compliant form using either spherical (e.g., latitude/longitude) or projected coordinates (e.g., rectilinear, such as State Plane Coordinate System). CrimeStat calculates a wide variety of spatial statistics and outputs tables, graphs, and graphical objects. A separate geographic information system (GIS), such as ArcGIS, MapInfo products, or Surfer, is required to open and view the graphical object files. Tables can be printed as text (.txt) files. Some CrimeStat modules (e.g., Crime Travel Demand module) require separate input files, and these files must be in dbf format.

CrimeStat runs on Windows computers. The trial runs, with 1,349 data points and 100 simulations on a three-year-old laptop, took about 15 seconds; however, during the run, other computer functions were markedly slower.

### Hardware

CrimeStat runs only on Windows systems (commonly called *personal computers* or PCs). Windows 7 is recommended, but CrimeStat will run on earlier versions of Windows as well. Minimum requirements to install and run CrimeStat are 256 megabytes (MB) of RAM and an 800-megahertz (MHz) processor computer, but an optimal configuration is 1 gigabyte (GB) of RAM and a 1.6-MHz or faster processor.

### Data

CrimeStat requires at least one and up to three input files. The primary file that specifies the locations of crime incidents is required. This file must include x- and y-coordinates in either latitude/longitude or projected values. Intensity and weight values are allowed, and each incident can have an associated time value. A secondary file can be supplied and is used for comparison with the primary file in the risk-adjusted nearest-neighbor clustering routine and the dual-kernel interpolation. The secondary file must be in the same format and units as the primary file. A third file, called a reference file, can be supplied or can be calculated by CrimeStat. The reference file is a grid file that overlays the study area and provides a means to visualize the grouping of events by zone. The grid can be regular or irregular (e.g., beat areas). CrimeStat can generate the grid if given the x- and y-coordinates for the lower-left and upper-right corners.

Prior to each run, the user must also specify measurement preferences, such as the type of distance measurement (direct, indirect, or network), and parameters for the area of study and the length of the street network.

*User Preparation*

A basic GIS background and knowledge of at least one GIS tool is required to view the output data. Criminology experience is needed to select the appropriate input. Experience with use of statistical tools in crime analysis is required to interpret the output. College-level statistical expertise is required to understand the theory behind the CrimeStat routines.

*Support*

A user's manual includes detailed instructions for installation and in-depth explanations with screen shots for each program feature. There is also a PowerPoint presentation and workbook, both of which are shorter than the full manual. Sample data sets are provided, and there is a fairly extensive built-in help function that essentially duplicates the quick guide. Some users recommended the three-day training course, but it does not appear that such training courses are currently available.

CrimeStat is available at Inter-University Consortium for Political and Social Research (undated [b]). The website includes download, documentation, and contact information.

## Operational Assessment

*Current Utility*

CrimeStat offers the law enforcement community and criminal justice researchers an option to obtain a large spectrum of statistical tools useful for crime analysis free of charge. Some CrimeStat functions are also available from a variety of commercial sources, such as ArcGIS and WinBUGS, but, for some routines, CrimeStat incorporates more interpolation methods. Major statistical packages, such as SAS and SPSS, do not include some of the CrimeStat routines. The CrimeStat output can be used for tactical crime analysis relating to crime patterns, crime series, and forecasting; strategic crime analysis relating to hot spots, problem solving, and geographic profiling; and operations analysis relating to patrol routes, patrol districts, and response times.

No registration process and no administrative privileges on a computer are required to download CrimeStat. Users must acknowledge compliance with a license agreement prior to program launch.

For experienced crime analysts who are familiar with the underlying statistical theory, installation and basic CrimeStat operational know-how can be accomplished in a few hours.

The data input procedure is not intuitive and requires careful reading of the documentation or training. Understanding the statistical theory in the program requires college-level knowledge of statistics. The output, in visual format using a separate GIS, is intuitive, but interpretation of the results is largely left to the user. Transferring the CrimeStat output to be inputted into a separate program is an additional step that can be burdensome for frequent or routine users.

CrimeStat Libraries are component objects that allow tool developers to directly program the functions in CrimeStat into other applications. Tool developers can download CrimeStat Libraries and accompanying documentation for CrimeStat Libraries from Inter-University Consortium for Political and Social Research (undated [b]).

### Potential Enhancements and Limitations

There are some known problems with CrimeStat, and the developer lists 11 of them in a separate readme file to alert the user and offer tips on workarounds. Developing CrimeStat as an extension to popular GIS, such as ArcMap, may draw more users because the need to open another program, a GIS, to view the CrimeStat output would be eliminated. The particular GIS user communities would gain an enhanced statistical capability. As such, the expense for creating such an extension should be borne or at least shared by the GIS developers. Another approach for enhancement would be to rewrite the libraries in Python so they could be used in ArcGIS and in automated processes developed with ModelBuilder.

### Potential Utility

The CrimeStat package of tools is unique and hence provides a new capability for the law enforcement community. Documentation is available, and crime analysts can adopt CrimeStat with little or no extra support. However, some users may not be able to attend a multiday training session or devote the time necessary to read through hundreds of pages of instructions. More users may be attracted to using the tool if more conveniently accessible support material, such as a free online training video, were available.

The release of CrimeStat version 4 was planned for 2013. That version will have expanded capabilities and extensive support material.

### Potential as a Commercial Product

The developer of CrimeStat has no plans to pursue commercialization of CrimeStat. The developer is a researcher who developed CrimeStat to provide spatial statistical tools to researchers and analysts.

### Impact

NIJ's investment in CrimeStat resulted in bringing an extensive array of statistical capabilities to the law enforcement community, some of which were not available with any other statistical software package. The tool is primarily of use to crime analysts, though the interpretation of CrimeStat output can influence operational decisions in particular cases. The detailed descriptions of the CrimeStat routines in the tool documentation may be of interest to criminology researchers.

Third-party applications can integrate CrimeStat routines with CrimeStat Libraries.

### Recommendations

The planned release of the next version of CrimeStat will address some user-identified issues. The planned update will include expanded documentation that will address the changes in the new version. These events can potentially make CrimeStat more attractive and enlarge the CrimeStat user base without further development action by NIJ. CrimeStat should continue to be featured in NIJ sources that publicize its geospatial software tools because it is a fully functional tool that runs on commonly available hardware, is well supported, and is being regularly used by crime analysts. Including CrimeStat in NIJ publicity on geospatial tools would increase its visibility to other potential users in the law enforcement community.

## Facility Cop

### Technical Assessment
#### Function
Facility Cop is a prison incident–mapping and database-creation software program. It was adapted from the School COP software program, discussed later in this chapter, and tailored for the correctional environment. Facility Cop allows the user to enter incident data for one or more facilities, view basic graphs and reports of the data, and view the incidents on a facility map provided by the user.

#### Software
Facility Cop is a stand-alone program. The user downloads the program and enters the password shown in the user's manual to launch the program. The user can change the password once the program is launched. The user clicks on the administrative function button to register facility maps and create a database framework. The facility maps must be in .bmp file format and are not required; however, if maps are not registered, the mapping functions are not available. The database framework allows the user to specify a range of options, such as the number of shifts, the types of weapons, and severity levels. The database framework selections become drop-down menus that the user can employ to input incident data to create the database. A large variety of reports, graphs, and mapping views are available as output.

#### Hardware
Facility Cop runs only on Windows 95 or a more recent version of Windows with at least 16 MB of RAM and 10 MB or more available hard disk space.

#### Data
Incident data are manually entered for each incident. Facility maps are provided by the user and must be in .bmp format. Instructions for creating a .bmp file using an existing map and a scanner are included in the user's manual.

### User Preparation

No special training is required to use Facility Cop. A high school education and basic computer skills are sufficient. The data-entry interface is straightforward and intuitive. Reports are intuitive and require no special training to interpret.

### Support

A user's manual includes instructions for installation and explanations with screen shots for each program feature. A sample facility map is provided, though the facility is a school rather than a correctional facility. Facility Cop is available at Temple University (undated [a]). The website includes download, documentation, and contact information.

## Operational Assessment

### Current Utility

Facility Cop provides the correctional community a simple-to-use tool to track incidents at one or more facilities. The tool requires no special training and can be mastered within an hour. The database terminology is tailored to a correctional environment so is easier to use than, say, a spreadsheet with the same information. The facility-mapping feature is unique, and the .bmp format makes the tool accessible to any facility.

The data-input procedure is intuitive, but it can be tedious and time-consuming to enter the individual data elements. Facility Cop is a stand-alone tool and, as such, has no networking capability.

### Potential Enhancements and Limitations

Facility Cop is a tool that can be used daily to track incidents at one or more correctional facilities. A database framework need be set up only once, and the tool can be up and running within minutes of installation. Because personal data for each person involved in an incident must be entered manually (e.g., name, birthdate, identification number), the data may be more prone to errors or inconsistencies with other databases than if such data could be automatically read from existing databases. This is a potential enhancement to Facility Cop.

As noted above, Facility Cop is a stand-alone program with no networking capabilities. With the increasing use of mobile devices, such as tablets, developing some capabilities to allow remote entry of incident data by multiple personnel could make Facility Cop more attractive to potential users. The potential benefits of such an enhancement would have to be balanced with cost and data security concerns.

### Potential Utility

Facility Cop provides basic incident reporting and mapping capabilities in an easy-to-use format. As such, it can be easily adapted by many facilities with no resource expenditure. Other record programs may provide some of the same capability, but the mapping capability appears unique.

### Potential as a Commercial Product

Temple University adapted School COP to be used in correctional facilities and called the adaptation Facility Cop. Currently, it is a free package, and there are no plans to commercialize it.

### Impact

NIJ's investment in Facility Cop resulted in a free, easy-to-use incident-mapping and database-creation software tool that requires only minutes to download and use. The documentation takes only a short time to work through before the user can begin entering incident data. Facility Cop incorporates labeling that is tailored for use by the correctional community. Correctional facilities that desire a mapping capability could adapt Facility Cop without expenditure of resources other than the time to enter the incidents in the database.

### Recommendations

Any improvements to Facility Cop should be tied to improvements to School COP because the former is a derivative of the latter. Any improvements to one tool are transferable to the other tool. For this reason, no further development actions are recommended for Facility Cop alone because pursuing any improvements in tandem is more-efficient use of NIJ funds. (See School COP recommendations.) Facility Cop should continue to be featured in NIJ sources that publicize its geospatial software tools because it is a fully functional tool that runs on commonly available hardware, has readily available support material, is being used by the law enforcement community, and requires no additional tethering software to run. Including Facility Cop in NIJ publicity on geospatial tools will increase its exposure to other potential users.

## GeoDaNet

### Technical Assessment
#### Function
GeoDaNet identifies clusters of crimes on networks and calculates distances based on street distance rather than straight-line distance.

#### Software
GeoDaNet software is currently available as an alpha release. The program can be used to compute and visualize spatial-analysis measures on undirected networks.[3] The alpha release version of GeoDaSpace can compute network (street distances[4]) and Euclidean distances, network and Euclidean distance accessibility measures, network and planar global K function and kernel density surface, network local K function, and local indicators of network-constrained clusters.

For the alpha release, the user must register (for free) on the ASU website to download GeoDaNet. Once the software is downloaded, the user launches the program and uses the resulting menu bar to access the GeoDaNet computational capabilities. He or she selects a function, such as distances, access measures, global K-Function, kernel density, local K-Function, and local indicators of network-constrained clusters. A pop-up window appears for the user to specify the required

---

[3]  A network is a graph that can be depicted with points that are called nodes and lines between nodes that are called edges. An edge represents a relationship between the connected nodes. When the edges represent symmetric relationships, the network is called undirected.

[4]  As used in this paragraph, *computer network distance*, also known as street distance, is the measurement of distance between two points based on the lengths of the streets that must be traversed to get from the first point to the second point. Street distance is also known as rectilinear distance or Manhattan distance. In contrast, the Euclidean distance between two points is the straight-line distance between the points.

inputs and an output file. Input and output file requirements depend on which GeoDaNet computational capabilities are selected. Once the inputs are specified, clicking the Compute button results in production of the output. Clicking the Visualization tab allows the user to select displays of the output.

### Hardware

GeoDaNet runs on Windows and Mac OS X. The recommended processor speed is 2.53 GHz. The recommended RAM to install and run is 2 GB. The recommended hard drive size to install and run is 10 GB (Windows XP requires 1.5 GB, Windows 7 requires 15 GB, Mac OS X 10.4 requires 3 GB, Mac OS X 10.5 requires 9 GB). In addition, a minimum display size of 13 inches (diagonal) with $800 \times 600$ resolution is recommended.

### Data

GeoDaNet input data must be in a .shp, .dbf, or .csv file with x- and y-coordinates. The user's manual contains detailed explanations of the input files required for each GeoDaNet computational capability. GeoDaNet outputs .shp, .dbf, and .csv files.

### User Preparations

GeoDaNet users are primarily crime analysts with knowledge of statistical modeling. Only experienced crime analysts with college-level statistics knowledge and expertise in the use of spatial statistics in crime analysis can specify the proper input, interpret the model output, and understand the underlying theory.

### Support

The GeoDaNet web page is user friendly. A user's manual describes each of the GeoDaNet functions, includes step-by-step instructions for the input sequences; provides sample data; and includes discussions to help the user understand the output. Slides are also available. In addition, a built-in help function displays explanations of errors when errors are encountered. GeoDaNet is available at GeoDa Center for Geospatial Analysis and Computation (undated [d]).

## Operational Assessment
### Current Utility
GeoDaNet is an alpha-release stand-alone software package that includes a variety of functions for computing and visualizing spatial-analysis measures on undirected networks. Other commercial software packages, such as SANET, contain some of the functionality in GeoDaNet, but no existing program contains all of the GeoDaNet functions. With the detailed user's manual, crime analysts with college-level statistics knowledge can use the GeoDaNet functions to generate various views of crime data. Interpretation of results is left to the user.

### Potential Enhancements and Limitations
GeoDaNet is in active development. Beta-test and final release versions are planned for the future. These future versions are being developed with non-NIJ funding and may contain additional functionality.

### Potential Utility
GeoDaNet is potentially useful to any researcher, criminologist, or analyst who wants to compute and visualize spatial-analysis measures on undirected networks. The user base for GeoDaNet may expand once a final version is released.

### Potential as a Commercial Product
The developer has no plans to turn GeoDaNet into a commercial product.

## Impact
GeoDaNet provides experienced crime analysts with a new no-cost capability to identify clusters of crimes on networks and calculate distances and other measures. The product, even in alpha release, has detailed documentation that makes it accessible to experienced crime analysts who take the time (about a day) to go through the manual. Such analysts need to already understand the role spatial statistics can play in crime analysis because the discussions to aid the user in understanding the output may not be adequate for a novice user.

### Recommendations

GeoDaNet is in active development, and ASU has a plan in place for this geospatial software tool—namely, a beta-test version and then a final release version. NIJ should include GeoDaNet in its publicity for NIJ-funded tools because it is a fully functional tool that runs on commonly available hardware, is well supported, and is being used by crime analysts. Including GeoDaNet in NIJ publicity on geospatial tools will increase its visibility to other potential users in the law enforcement community.

## GeoDaSpace

### Technical Assessment
*Function*

GeoDaSpace enables analysts to estimate spatial regression models. It outputs views of crime as a function of environmental design characteristics and other variables.

*Software*

GeoDaSpace software is currently available as a beta release. The program implements models that control for both spatial autocorrelation and heteroskedasticity.[5]

For the beta release, the user must register (for free) on the ASU website to download GeoDaSpace. Downloading requires the user to proceed through a multiple-click process. The process is straightforward but does require that the user pay attention and answer each query. A one-click download is planned for future releases. Once downloaded, the user opens the program and selects a data input file. The user specifies the input variables. The X variable can be specified via choices in a built-in drop-down menu. The dependent Y variable can be specified by dragging the choices from a drop-down menu to the appropriate box in the GeoDaSpace main menu screen. The user may also provide inputs for model weights and kernel weights and specify the model

---

[5]   A group of statistical or probability distributions that have nonidentical variances is called heteroskedastic.

parameters (e.g., model type from four choices: standard, spatial log, spatial error, or spatial lag + error). Clicking the Run button results in near-instant display of an output summary that the user can save as a text file. Output files are in .dbf or .csv format.

### Hardware

GeoDaSpace runs on Windows and Mac OS X. The recommended processor is 1.0 GHz (300 MHz for Windows XP; 1 GHz for Windows 7; 867 MHz for Mac OS X), but the software will run on a slower processor as well. The recommended RAM to install and run is 512 MB (64 MB for Windows XP; 1 GB for Windows 7; 512 MB for Mac OS X 10.5), but the software will run on less RAM. The recommended hard drive size to install and run is 10 GB (1.5 GB for Windows XP; 15 GB for Windows 7; 3 GB for Mac OS X 10.4; 9 GB for Mac OS X 10.5). In addition, a minimum display size of 10 inches (diagonal) with 800 × 600 resolution is recommended.

### Data

GeoDaSpace input data must be in .shp format or a .dbf or .csv file with x- and y-coordinates. The data input file must be created using other programs prior to running GeoDaSpace.

### User Preparations

GeoDaSpace users are primarily analysts who study long-term crime trends. Users must have college-level expertise in spatial statistics, thoroughly understand statistical modeling, and have experience in the use of statistical methods in crime analysis. These qualifications are necessary to specify the proper input, interpret the model output, and understand the underlying theory.

### Support

The GeoDaSpace web page is very user friendly. Technical notes are available. A user's manual is being written. A built-in help function is available and guides the user through selecting appropriate input files.

GeoDaSpace is available at GeoDa Center for Geospatial Analysis and Computation (undated [e]).

## Operational Assessment

### *Current Utility*

GeoDaSpace is a beta release software package that includes spatial diagnostic tests to detect whether spatial structure is present in the data and needs to be controlled for along with nonspatial diagnostic tests for nonnormal errors and multicollinearity. Other commercial software packages, such as R and Stata, contain some of the functionality in GeoDaSpace, but no existing program duplicates GeoDaSpace functionality. In particular, existing software packages do not offer a user-friendly point-and-click graphical user interface (GUI) like GeoDaSpace's. With the limited documentation of the GeoDaSpace beta release, primary users are experienced crime analysts with college-level statistics expertise who understand the role of spatial statistics in crime analysis.

### *Potential Enhancements and Limitations*

GeoDaSpace is in active development. Final release versions are planned for the future. These future versions are being developed with non-NIJ funding and may contain additional functionality.

### *Potential Utility*

GeoDaSpace is potentially useful to any researcher, criminologist, or analyst who understands the use of standard nonspatial and new spatial estimators for multivariate regression models (continuous dependent variables) with and without heteroskedasticity (nonnormal errors) in crime analysis. The user base for GeoDaSpace may expand once final release versions with up-to-date documentation and training are available.

### *Potential as a Commercial Product*

The developer has no plans to turn GeoDaSpace into a commercial product.

## Impact

GeoDaSpace provides experienced crime analysts who are versed in spatial statistical application in crime analysis with a no-cost spatial regression modeling capability. The product, even in beta release, is quite fast but lacks up-to-date documentation (which is now in progress).

### Recommendations

GeoDaSpace is in active development. ASU has a plan in place for this geospatial software tool—namely, final release versions along with updated and expanded documentation. NIJ should include GeoDaSpace in its publicity for NIJ-funded tools because it is a fully functional tool, runs on commonly available hardware, and is being used by crime analysts. Including GeoDaSpace in NIJ publicity on geospatial tools will increase its visibility to other potential users in the law enforcement community.

## Geographic Profiler

### Technical Assessment

*Function*

Geographic Profiler generates the probable location of a serial offender's anchor point based on locations of his or her previous crimes. Geographic Profiler outputs the results as .csv, .dbf, .kml, and .shp files that can be viewed on maps using a separate GIS. The output maps show probability density in color-coded triangular areas, with red indicating high probability, yellow indicating medium probability, and green indicating lower probability.

*Software*

Geographic Profiler uses historical data to calculate a probability density representing the chances that an offender with a particular anchor point would commit an offense at different locations. Geographic Profiler outputs file-mapping data as coarse results, fine results, historical crimes, and prior anchor points in .csv, .dbf, .kml, and .shp file formats. In addition, estimated offender average offense distance, historical crimes, prior anchor points, and prior distribution of average offense distance are output in .csv and .txt files. The coarse results show color-coded triangles that encompass larger geographic areas (e.g., higher-elevation views on Google Earth), and the fine results show color-coded triangles that encompass smaller geographic areas (e.g., lower-elevation views on Google Earth). Depending on a user's computer setup, clicking on the output file can display the map. For example, with an established Internet connection, clicking on the .kml output file for coarse results will display the results on Google Earth. The user can use Google Earth capabilities to navigate and zoom in on areas of interest. Yellow pushpins show the crime sites. The Google Earth maps can be saved to the user's computer. On a four-year-old laptop, the Google Earth maps took a couple of minutes to display.

Geographic Profiler run time is extremely long. Duplicating the example in the user's manual (seven crimes in the series being considered, 2,000 solved crimes, 500-foot map bandwidth, and using U.S. census data for Baltimore, Maryland) on a four-year-old laptop dedicated to this single task took just over 33.5 hours to complete. During the run, the computer could not be used for any other task without crashing. The developer cites a run time of 16.5 hours for the identical run on a fast computer, so run times can vary considerably depending on the computer's specifications. A helpful gauge of how the run is progressing is built into the tool.

### Hardware

The developer states that Geographic Profiler runs on any version of Windows PCs with no explicit minimum processor speed or memory requirements. However, as described above, Geographic Profiler runs will take longer on computers with less processing power, less available RAM, or less of both processing power and RAM.

### Data

Geographic Profiler requires four types of user-provided data. First, it requires locations of the crime series being considered. Second, it requires historical data containing the locations of solved crimes similar to the crime series being considered, along with the anchor points of the offender in each solved crime. Third, the program requires the locations of a large and robust collection of crimes that are representative of the distribution of crimes similar to the series crime throughout the jurisdiction. Crimes included in this third file need not be solved crimes. Finally, the user must choose a prior distribution for the location of the offender's anchor by either using data from the U.S. census or using the locations of known anchor points from prior offenders. The four input data files can be in plain text, .dbf, or .csv format. Location data must be in latitude/longitude. Input data structures with examples are described in detail in the user's manual and in built-in help screens. If U.S. census data is selected, Geographic Profiler provides an automatic link to download the required census data.

For practical purposes, a user must be able to automatically generate the solved-crime files and the robust collection of crimes in the jurisdiction from existing databases, such as an RMS. Manual generation of these two required input files would make Geographic Profiler very burdensome to use.

### User Preparations

A college education and basic computer skills are required to run Geographic Profiler.[6] The interfaces are straightforward and the support material is easy to follow, but selecting input files is not intuitive. The user must consult the user's manual to learn how to create and select appropriate input files and run the program. Experience in crime analysis is required to understand and interpret the results, although the maps are intuitive to read. College-level mathematics and statistics are required to understand the underlying theory. Therefore, the developer recommends a college-level education to use the tool.

### Support

A detailed user's manual explains the history of the program, the algorithms used, and detailed instructions on how to run the model. Explanations of the output can help the user interpret the resulting maps.

Geographic Profiler is available at O'Leary (2012). Tool documentation is also available on the website.

---

[6] The college education requirement was determined by statements by the tool developer and our independent assessment.

## Operational Assessment

### Current Utility

Geographic Profiler is currently a fully functional prototype. It uses a new algorithm to compute a prioritized search area for a serial offender based on the locations of the offender's crimes, locations of solved crimes, distributions of crime in the jurisdiction, and a prior distribution of the offender's anchor (e.g., distribution based on census data or distribution based on locations of known anchor points from prior offenders). Geographic profiling maps are available from other sources using other algorithms (e.g., CrimeStat, Rigel Analyst, Dragnet). To date, the results of Geographic Profiler match but are not consistently and convincingly more accurate than geographic maps available through other sources. Geographic Profiler offers the law enforcement community another tool that may produce a different view of the probable location of the offender's anchor point. As such, it can be used to establish robustness of results from several sources. The main drawback of Geographic Profiler (the prototype) is its long run time. This characteristic makes the tool impractical for some situations because law enforcement agencies may not be able to set aside a computer for one or more days to make a single Geographic Profiler run.

### Potential Enhancements and Limitations

The primary limitation to Geographic Profiler is its long run times. It is unclear whether run times can be significantly decreased with software modifications. Evidence that the existing algorithm or a modification of the existing algorithm consistently and convincingly produces more-accurate results would make Geographic Profiler more attractive to the law enforcement community as well. With such an improvement, potential users would be more willing to accommodate the long run times.

### Potential Utility

Primary users of Geographic Profiler are crime analysts. Crime analysts use a variety of tools, and Geographic Profiler can be one of them, but the long run times may make this tool an unlikely routine choice among other programs that offer similar priority maps. Geographic Profiler can be used to establish robustness of results in particular cases.

As computing power improves in standard computers, the run times may decrease as computers are upgraded at law enforcement agencies. Hence, the run times of Geographic Profiler may decrease in the future without any modifications to the code, although it is unlikely that run times would be reduced significantly in the near future.

Researchers developing tools and capabilities for law enforcement may find Geographic Profiler useful to make comparisons among approaches for geographic profiling.

### Potential as a Commercial Product

The current version of Geographic Profiler is a well-functioning prototype. Professional development time would be required to turn Geographic Profiler into a commercial product. The developer has no plans to pursue commercialization of Geographic Profiler.

### Impact

Geographic Profiler offers the law enforcement community another tool with a new approach to calculating probability density that an offender with a particular anchor point would commit an offense at various locations. The long run times associated with the Geographic Profiler prototype may limit its user base.

### Recommendations

Geographic Profiler is a fully functional tool that runs on commonly available hardware and has excellent support material. However, long run times may deter potential users from adopting the tool. Hence, we recommend a basic cost/benefit analysis to determine whether a small additional investment can significantly reduce run times (a reduction of 50 percent or more). If significant run-time decreases are not feasible with software modifications, NIJ should not take further actions for Geographic Profiler because the algorithms may simply require a high level of computing power. If that is the case, the run times will decrease only as computers become more powerful. NIJ should include Geographic Profiler in promotions and publicity of other NIJ-funded geospatial tools because it is a fully functional tool that crime analysts can use when data sets are small or run times are inconsequential.

## Mobile Semi-Automated 3-D Tool

### Technical Assessment

*Function*

Mobile Semi-Automated 3-D is a system that provides location and movement information about first responders. The responders can receive complete three-dimensional (3-D) models of indoor environments (e.g., the interior of a building), including the ability to find the shortest route to any location. Mobile Semi-Automated 3-D can automatically update routes to take into account blockages that may occur. A real-time evacuation simulation is incorporated in the tool. The evacuation simulation can also be updated to reflect environmental changes or unforeseen circumstances. Visualizations and schedules are automatically generated to provide actions to assist decisionmakers. Commanders can use the information to direct responders.

*Software*

This review is based solely on information provided directly by the developer and by a representative designated by the developer because no users responded to RAND requests for input and the developer was not able to specify download arrangements for the study team to observe this tool during the time frame of the study. Mobile Semi-Automated 3-D is not available for download or installation directly by potential users. Potential users are instructed to contact the developer to make arrangements because downloads must be handled in conjunction with the developer's staff. A website provides developer contact information. For areas in which the developer and the developer's representative provided different information, we either do not address them or review them using the most–recently received information.

Mobile Semi-Automated 3-D uses open-source software. For the automated 3-D graph generation from computer-aided design (CAD) files, ArcGIS or another GIS package should be used. The Esri ArcGIS desktop license costs $300.

### Hardware

Conflicting information regarding hardware requirements was provided by the developer and the developer's designated representative. Hence, it is unclear what hardware constraints apply to this tool.

### Data

Street databases are provided for testing. The developer can provide test data for several buildings, including all buildings on the University of North Carolina at Charlotte campus, upon agreement. User-provided data compatible with Mobile Semi-Automated 3-D include building layout drawings and annotations, such as room numbering, schedules, and purpose. Spatial data, maps, images, and street routes should be in standard GIS formats. Categorical data can be in Structured Query Language (SQL). Most output is visual in nature and viewable via GIS, but evacuation plans can be output as categorical lists or schedules.

### User Preparations

The required user preparation is unclear because the developer was not able to specify download arrangements for the study team to observe this tool during the time frame of this study. The developer states that Mobile Semi-Automated 3-D is designed to be used by emergency responders, so users would have emergency response, search and routing, and emergency evacuation training.

### Support

The developer states that, at the time of this geospatial tool evaluation study, documentation for Mobile Semi-Automated 3-D was undergoing review.[7] Potential users are instructed to contact the developers to make the required arrangements to download and use the tool. Test data for several buildings and all buildings on the University of North Carolina at Charlotte campus are available from the developer upon agreement. Updates are provided after each exercise or evaluation, but only within a collaborative group. Membership requirements for the collaborative group are not specified. Documentation was not available for this review.

---

[7]   Documentation was not available for this study.

## Operational Assessment
### Current Utility
The developer states that primary uses of Mobile Semi-Automated 3-D to date have been user training exercises.

### Potential Enhancements and Limitations
The developer states that the current version of Mobile Semi-Automated 3-D includes some indoor location capability but that this capability is not robust, particularly for power-outage situations. The improved version is incomplete, so completing the more-robust automated indoor location capability is a potential enhancement. Mobile Semi-Automated 3-D can also be enhanced with more-graceful switching between communication modes (Wi-Fi, cell network, police radio).

### Potential Utility
The developer has received expressions of interest from the University of North Carolina system. This system has 17 locations and some police forces. The developer is interested in following up on leads to police forces that NIJ may provide. The developer states that Mobile Semi-Automated 3-D can be used for broader emergency planning and for general people-movement planning and scheduling in crowded neighborhoods. The developer has begun a project to apply Mobile Semi-Automated 3-D to the latter application.

### Potential as a Commercial Product
The developer is filing an invention disclosure and is looking into commercialization. The primary barriers to turning Mobile Semi-Automated 3-D into a commercial product are the time and effort required of the developers to transform the tool into a commercial product.

## Impact
Because the study team did not view the tool or receive any input from users, no impact to the law enforcement community or research community was observed.

### Recommendations

Mobile Semi-Automated 3-D is a system that provides location and movement information about first responders. During the time frame of this study, we were unable to confirm that access to the tool is feasible. The developer states that Mobile Semi-Automated 3-D will be available to police departments and other agencies that show a need for the program. The developer will determine availability on a case-by-case basis. Hence, we recommend that NIJ confirm tool access.

## Near Repeat Calculator

### Technical Assessment
#### *Function*

Near Repeat Calculator generates estimates of increased probability that crime will take place within distances and time frames of recent crimes. It generates tables that show the increased likelihoods (in increased percentages) for varying distances (in meters or feet) and times (in days), starting with a repeat crime at the exact same location within one day (24 hours) of a recent crime and then extending outward in distance and forward in time.

#### *Software*

Near Repeat Calculator is a stand-alone program. It uses historical crime data provided by the user to calculate the probabilities that an incident will occur within specific distances and time frames of historical incidents. The user must provide x- and y-coordinate values for the location of recent crimes along with the date of the crimes. Input format is structured in that the program can read only comma-separated value (.csv) input files (e.g., from Microsoft Excel) and locations must be expressed in rectilinear coordinates. The user can specify data distance in feet or meters and choose distances to be computed in Euclidean (straight-line) distances or Manhattan (right-angle) distances. The program outputs summary statistical data in Microsoft Excel–generated .csv files and web pages (hypertext markup language, or HTML, often with an extension of .html). Results significant at the

0.01 level are shown in red, and results significant at the 0.05 level are shown in brown.

### Hardware

Near Repeat Calculator runs only on Windows PCs. The program took a couple of minutes to initiate on a six-year old laptop but runs much more quickly on a newer computer. The run times vary depending on the number of crime records—the more records, the longer the run time, up to an hour for 10,000 records on a modern laptop. Crashes are more likely with larger numbers of crime records. The maximum number of crime records that can be analyzed within a given run is 10,000.

### Data

The user provides historical data in .csv format with one crime per line. The x- and y-coordinate values (from a projected coordinate system, such as State Plane Coordinate System) indicate the crime location. Near Repeat Calculator is not compatible with latitude/longitude coordinates. If input data are provided in latitude/longitude, the program will run, but the distance calculations will be less accurate. Each line of the input file represents one crime with the x-coordinate value in the first column, the y-coordinate value in the second column, and the date in the third column. For practical purposes, the user needs a program (e.g., record management system [RMS]) that can automatically generate input files. Without automatic generation of input files, the tool becomes impractical because of the time it would take to manually create an input file in the correct format.

### User Preparations

A high school education and basic computer skills are required to run the program. Crime-analysis experience is also required because the user must know a priori what the program does and why he or she is running it; there is limited guidance in the support material that explains the purpose of the software or what it does. In addition, the user must be able to prepare input files in the format required. Near Repeat Calculator output reports are self-explanatory and are in table format. An HTML browser is required to view the HTML web-page output.

### Support

A short user's manual provides installation instructions with explanations accompanied by screen shots. A built-in help function also explains the program features. These support materials contain limited discussions on what the program does. Interpretation of the results is left to the user.

Near Repeat Calculator is available at Temple University (undated [b]). The user must enter an email address to download the tool.

## Operational Assessment

### Current Utility

Near Repeat Calculator provides a capability that calculates the increased probability that new crime will occur within specified distances and time frames of historical crime. The user need provide only locations and dates of recent crimes as input. The tool is easy to use and provides self-explanatory output reports.

Near Repeat Calculator calculates the odds ratio of repeat and near-repeat space-time crime patterns. Statistical significance is established through a Monte Carlo approach—the program randomly permutes the dates of crimes a specific number of times depending on significance level requested by the user. It compares the nearest spatio-temporal distances in the actual data with those in the permuted data to estimate increased probability.

Near Repeat Calculator output can help the law enforcement community understand near-repeat patterns. Understanding the additional risk of crime to areas surrounding a crime site can help law enforcement agencies plan crime-prevention activity. The developer indicates that the tool is in use by many crime analysts and is being included in some training material.

### Potential Enhancements and Limitations

Many popular systems used by crime analysts, such as Google Earth, Keyhole Markup Language (KML, with .kml files), and SPIDER use latitude/longitude location data. Near Repeat Calculator's incompatibility with latitude/longitude may make this tool less attractive to crime analysts whose data is in the now-common latitude/longitude format. Because conversion between latitude/longitude and rectilinear is nontrivial, developing a latitude/longitude readability enhancement may lead to many more users. Latitude/longitude compatibility is a potential enhancement to the program.

Making Near Repeat Calculator compatible with more input formats, such as common RMS formats, could allow for automatic generation of input files and thereby also increase its user base.

Near Repeat Calculator has a built-in minimum temporal resolution of 24 hours (one day). Although this may not be a limitation in most cases, the one-day fidelity means that the user will not be able to distinguish between true next-day (within 24 hours) crime and crime sprees in close proximity and short time spans (e.g., three break-ins on the same block within an hour). Developing an enhancement that can handle a time input could allow for finer fidelities but needs to be balanced with longer run times.

Near Repeat Calculator can accommodate only one type of crime at a time. Extending the capability to handle multiple crime types would allow for comparison among crime types.

The Near Repeat Calculator has a built-in nonfixable characteristic, namely its nontraditional Monte Carlo approach used to calculate estimates of increased likelihood. Specifically, it randomly permutes the dates of the crimes a given number of times (20 for 0.05 significance, 100 for 0.01 significance, and 1,000 for 0.001 significance) and compares the nearest spatiotemporal distances in the actual data with those in the permuted data to estimate the increased likelihoods. The increased likelihoods seem to be deemed "significant" to a particular level if they have shorter distances than the other permuted data runs. Some scientists believe that the use of permutations to set background levels and determining significance as described above is atypical, though not incorrect. Near Repeat Calculator is being tested under a postdevelopment award (award 2012-IJ-CX-0039). The results of this follow-on examination of the tool should indicate the long-term role it could play in crime analysis.

### Potential Utility

Primary users of Near Repeat Calculator are crime analysts. The tool has also been used by the military to analyze improvised explosive device (IED) attacks on coalition forces in Iraq.

### Potential as a Commercial Product

The software, code, and algorithms used in Near Repeat Calculator are in the public domain. The developer has no plans to pursue commercialization of the program.

## Impact

Near Repeat Calculator is a free tool that provides estimates of increased likelihood that crime will occur within windows of time and distance of recent crime. Commercial products, such as PredPol, offer similar functionality. Near Repeat Calculator provides the law enforcement community with another tool to address crime prevention. Its inability to read input formats other than a structured .csv file and its incompatibility with latitude/longitude may be factors limiting a larger user base.

## Recommendations

Currently, Near Repeat Calculator is a fully functional tool that is free to users, runs on commonly available hardware, and has support material adequate for experienced crime analysts to use the tool. The tool has a few drawbacks that, if remedied, could make the tool attractive to more crime analysts. We recommend a basic cost/benefit analysis to determine whether a small additional investment to address these drawbacks by expanding the types of input files that Near Repeat Calculator can read, developing latitude/longitude compatibility, and allowing for more than one crime type to be considered will result in a larger user base. We make this recommendation because such a cost/benefit analysis would indicate whether NIJ has an opportunity to efficiently deliver more benefits from Near Repeat Calculator to the law enforcement community. Such a cost/benefit study should include an investigation of interest by the defense community because the tool has been used by the military to analyze IED attacks in Iraq. Shared funding of Near Repeat Calculator enhancements would benefit both the law enforcement and defense communities by providing a more versatile analysis tool applicable in both realms. The program should continue to be featured in NIJ sources that publicize its geospatial software tools.

## OpenGeoDa

### Technical Assessment
*Function*
NIJ funding extended OpenGeoDa functionality to include spatial data analysis of crime data across time. Prior to the extension, analysts could use OpenGeoDa to perform cross-sectional analysis.

*Software*
The NIJ-funded time-enabling functionality in OpenGeoDa includes maps to detect outliers, scatterplots, parallel coordinate plots, box plots, histograms, local cluster maps, and global clustering.

Download of OpenGeoDa requires registration (for free) and administrative privileges on the computer on which the software is to reside. The download sequence is available on the website and is straightforward. Once downloaded, the user can run OpenGeoDa, which displays a floating toolbar with ten menu items. The analyst uses the File menu to open an .shp file containing the crime data to be used in the analysis. The Tools menu contains tools that allow the user to perform functions, such as create weights, create .shp files from ASCII, and import and export .csv files. The user selects the table options from the Tables menu, maps from the Maps menu, plots (e.g., scatter, box) from the Explore menu, spatial options (e.g., spatial autocorrelation analysis) from the Space menu, and methods to be used (e.g., regression analysis) from the Methods menu. The Options menu allows the user to select various display options and save file features. The Help menu is a built-in help capability. Finally, the OpenGeoDa menu contains administrative information, such as version number. OpenGeoDa is intuitive, and, as long as the analyst knows which tables, maps, and methods are most appropriate for the analysis being performed, the tool is easy to use. The selection of appropriate tables, maps, and methods, as well as the interpretation of the results, is left to the user, so he or she needs to be thoroughly familiar with the use of the available functions in a law enforcement application.

### Hardware

OpenGeoDa runs on versions of Windows XP or more-recent versions of Windows, Mac OS X or more-recent versions of the Mac operating system, and Linux. A minimum processor speed of 1.0 GHz is recommended (300 MHz for Windows XP; 1 GHZ for Windows 7; 867 MHz for Mac OS X 10.5), but OpenGeoDa will run on slower processors. A minimum of 512 MB RAM is recommended to install and run (64 MB for Windows XP; 1 GB for Windows 7; 512 MB for Mac OS X 10.5), but OpenGeoDa will run on systems with less RAM. A minimum hard drive capacity of 10 GB is recommended to install and run (Windows XP requires 1.5 GB, Windows 7 requires 15 GB, Mac OS X 10.4 requires 3 GB, and Mac OS X 10.5 requires 9 GB). A 13-inch (diagonal) display with a minimum of $800 \times 600$ resolution and RGB color and contrast is required.

### Data

OpenGeoDa requires aggregated crime data. These aggregated files have to be provided by the user and created using a separate program. Input files are .shp files. Output files are .shp or .csv files.

### User Preparation

OpenGeoDa is designed to be used by crime analysts. College-level statistics is required to understand the underlying routines. Crime-analysis experience and knowledge of statistical methods are needed to create the required input, select the appropriate input options, and interpret the output.

### Support

An OpenGeoDa overview includes screen shots of the options available for each menu. A video is also available. Sample data are available to test the various functions and can be used to determine the formatting and components of data required in an input file. The developer states that there are more than 70,000 users of previous versions of OpenGeoDa (without the NIJ-funded time dimension functionality) and that many of these believe that OpenGeoDa is intuitive enough to not require a user's manual.

OpenGeoDa is available at GeoDa Center for Geospatial Analysis and Computation (undated [d]).

## Operational Assessment
### Current Utility
According to the developer, there are 70,000 users of previous versions of this functionality. Those users are likely to be users of OpenGeoDa with time dimension extensions as well. The NIJ-funded time dimension extensions were only recently released, so no users of this feature were available in the time frame of this study.

### Potential Enhancements and Limitations
The software is in active development. Additional statistical and mapping views would offer the criminologist a wider spectrum of tools to analyze crime data. Such potential enhancements include calendar and heat maps. ASU is planning to improve the performance of some routines using non-NIJ funds. OpenGeoDa requires aggregated crime data. The data aggregation has to be performed using a separate program. This is a nonfixable limitation of OpenGeoDa.

### Potential Utility
OpenGeoDa is an intuitive program for experienced criminologists with statistical expertise. It will be attractive to this target user group.

### Potential as a Commercial Product
The developer has no plans to turn OpenGeoDa into a commercial product.

## Impact
The NIJ-funded enhancement to OpenGeoDa gave the existing large crime-analyst community of OpenGeoDa users the capability to analyze crime data across time.

### Recommendations

ASU already has plans to improve the performance of some routines in OpenGeoDa. NIJ should include this functionality in its publicity for NIJ-funded geospatial software tools because it is a fully functional tool that runs on commonly available hardware and is being used by crime analysts. The previous versions of OpenGeoDa have a very large user base. These users of past versions are unlikely to need additional support material to use the enhanced functionality. Including OpenGeoDa in NIJ publicity on geospatial tools will increase the tool's visibility to other potential users in the law enforcement community.

## Python Spatial Analysis Library

### Technical Assessment
#### Function

PySAL is a Python (programming-language) library of spatial-analysis functions. NIJ-funded routines that are in the library include local cluster detection for polygons, cluster statistics for crimes on streets, computation of street distances between points and crime locations, spatial regression modeling, and spatial diagnostic tests for probit models. NIJ-funded PySAL functionality is integrated in applications, such as NIJ-funded GeoDaSpace, GeoDaNet, ArcGIS 10.2 PySAL Tool, and CAST.

#### Software

PySAL is a collection of spatial-analysis routines written in the Python programming language. Its primary users are tool developers rather than members of the law enforcement community. Tool developers can use the PySAL routines that incorporate spatial statistics algorithms as building blocks to more efficiently develop tool functionality. The law enforcement community most commonly uses spatial-analysis functions in PySAL indirectly through tools that use PySAL functions as building blocks. Table 3.1 shows the names of PySAL routines developed with NIJ funding and the names of NIJ-funded geospatial software tools that incorporate the PySAL routines.

**Table 3.1**
**Incorporation of PySAL Routines**

| PySAL Routine | Geospatial Software Tool | | | | |
| --- | --- | --- | --- | --- | --- |
| | ArcGIS 10.2 PySAL Tool | CAST | GeoDaNet | GeoDaSpace | OpenGeoDa |
| Local cluster detection for polygons | X | X | | | X |
| LISA Markov statistic for cluster persistence over time | | X | | | |
| Cluster statistics for crimes on streets | | | X | | |
| Computation of street distances between points (such as homes) and crimes | | | X | | |
| Spatial regression modeling | X | | | X | |
| Spatial diagnostic tests for probit models | | | | | |

NOTE: LISA = local indicators of spatial association.

Three free software packages are required to use PySAL directly. These are Python 2.5 or later, NumPy 1.3 or later, and SciPy 0.7 or later. Although PySAL's primary users are tool developers, crime analysts with Python programming expertise and an understanding of how spatial statistics can be used in crime analysis can use PySAL routines directly.

### Hardware

PySAL runs on Windows, Mac OS X, and Linux systems. A minimum 10-inch display is required.

### Data

PySAL input data must be in ASCII format. PySAL output is also in ASCII format.

### User Preparations

PySAL is a collection of routines designed to be used by tool developers. Expertise in the Python programming language at the high school level is required to use PySAL routines. The user must also have college-level spatial statistics expertise to understand the PySAL algorithms.

### Support

PySAL is intended to be used by tool developers. A user's manual for tool developers is available. Because the law enforcement community is not expected to be a direct user of PySAL, no support material aimed at crime analysts is available.

PySAL has an error-resolution process. When there are errors in PySAL, a log is generated that allows the user to trace the details of the problem.

PySAL is available at GeoDa Center for Geospatial Analysis and Computation (undated [g]).

## Operational Assessment
### Current Utility

PySAL is a library of routines written in the Python programming language. The PySAL routines have been used to develop geospatial software tools that are used by the law enforcement community. See Table 3.1 for specific geospatial tools developed by ASU using PySAL routines as building blocks. Tool developers are the targeted users of PySAL. The PySAL algorithms funded by NIJ are in active development. The alpha test versions were recently released, so not enough time has passed to identify or ascertain user experience.

### Potential Enhancements and Limitations

PySAL is designed in modular format to facilitate code extensions. Some of the Python-only code in PySAL is slower than C++ implementation,[8] but Python is easier to learn and use than C++. For some of the ASU geospatial software tools that incorporated PySAL routines in which C++ or C implementations were found to be faster than Python, ASU wrapped Python code around embedded C++ or C routines for better performance.[9]

### Potential Utility

Potential PySAL users include geospatial tool developers, advanced crime analysts in universities, government agencies, and police departments with experience in customizing software.

### Potential as a Commercial Product

There are no plans to commercialize PySAL. The Berkeley Software Distribution (BSD) license defines parameters for conversion of PySAL to a commercial product. BSD license parameters can be found at Open Source Initiative (undated).

### Impact

ASU has used PySAL routines to develop geospatial software tools. At the time of writing, there had been at least 1,386 downloads of PySAL, so other developers may be using these routines as well.

---

[8]    C++ is an intermediate-level programming language.

[9]    C is a general-purpose programming language.

### Recommendations

PySAL is a library of spatial statistical routines that tool developers can use to build tools. PySAL documentation is written for tool developers. ASU continues to improve PySAL using non-NIJ funding. We recommend that NIJ continue to feature PySAL in NIJ sources that publicize its geospatial software tools because PySAL is a collection of fully functional routines that can facilitate geospatial tool development.

## School COP

### Technical Assessment
#### *Function*
School COP is a school incident–mapping and database-creation software program. It allows the user to enter incident data for one or more schools, view basic graphs and reports of the data, and view the incidents on school maps provided by the user.

#### *Software*
School COP is a stand-alone program. The user downloads the program and enters the password shown in the user's manual to launch the program. The user can change the password once the program is launched. The user clicks the administrative function button to register school maps and create a database framework. The school maps must be in bitmap (.bmp) format and are not required; however, if maps are not registered, the mapping functions are not available. Any number of maps to any level of detail can be registered (e.g., floor plan of each building, school grounds). The database framework allows the user to specify a range of options, such as the types of incidents, the types of weapons, and severity levels. These options become drop-down lists for each incident report. Users can then input incident data to create the database. A large variety of reports, graphs, and mapping views are available as output.

### Hardware

School COP runs only on Windows systems (PCs). Windows 98 or a more recent version of Windows is required. In addition, 20 MB of RAM and 16 MB of hard disk capacity are required to install and run.

### Data

Incident data are manually entered for each incident. Any school maps to be used must be provided by the user in .bmp format. The user's manual includes instructions on how to create a .bmp file for an existing map.

### User Preparation

A high school education and basic computer skills are required to use the program.[10] The data-entry interface is straightforward and intuitive. Reports are intuitive and require no special training to interpret. The developer recommends reading the user's manual before using the tool. Reading the user's manual requires about an hour.

### Support

The user's manual includes instructions for installation and explanations with screen shots for each program feature. A sample facility map is provided.

School COP is available at School COP Software (undated [a]). The website includes download, documentation, a training video,[11] and contact information.

## Operational Assessment
### Current Utility

School COP provides schools and school districts a simple-to-use tool to track incidents at one or more schools. The tool requires no special training and can be mastered within minutes by anyone with a high

---

[10] The high school education requirement was determined by statements by the tool developer, input from users, and our independent assessment. Basic computer skills include such skills as being able to navigate the internet and follow download instructions, comprehend how to create a login and password, enter text into a template, and save files.

[11] The training video was funded by a follow-on contract between the developer and the COPS office.

school education and basic computer skills. The tool is tailored to a school environment, so is easier to use than, say, a spreadsheet with the same information. The mapping feature is unique, and the .bmp format makes the tool accessible to any school because a school map in .bmp format can be easily created by scanning a school floor plan and saving the scan as a .bmp file.

Although the primary users for School COP are schools, the tool can also be used to track incidents by school districts, summer camps, and any program where students gather.

The data-input procedure is intuitive, but it can be tedious to enter some data elements. School COP is a stand-alone tool and, as such, has no networking capability.

School COP benefited from a follow-on contract (funded by the Community Oriented Policing Services [COPS] office rather than by NIJ) to add new features and to market and disseminate the tool. That effort likely resulted in more users. The new features that are available in the current version (version 1.3) of School COP but were not in the NIJ-funded version (version 1.2) are the ability to add activities (in addition to incidents), archiving, automatic generation of an incident identification number each time a new incident is created, and a utility to merge multiple School COP databases.

At the present, the developer states that the tool is downloaded an average of 50 times per month.

### Potential Enhancements and Limitations

School COP is a tool that can be used daily to track incidents at a school. A database framework need be set up only once, and the tool can be up and running within minutes of installation. Because data for each person involved in an incident must be entered manually, the data may be more prone to errors or inconsistencies with other databases than if such data could be automatically read from existing databases. For example, if student data could be automatically downloaded to School COP, teachers or others entering incident data would not have to retrieve and enter the student's identification number, address, contact information, and other repeated information. Developing an interface for automatic downloading of student directories is a potential enhancement to School COP.

School COP is a stand-alone program with no networking capabilities. This was a deliberate development decision to maximize information security. More than a decade has passed since the stand-alone decision was made. With the advancements of information security options and increasing use of mobile devices, such as tablets and laptops, developing some capabilities to allow remote entry of incident data by multiple personnel may make School COP more attractive to schools with such technology.

### Potential Utility

School COP provides basic incident reporting and mapping capabilities in an easy-to-use format. As such, it can be easily adopted by many schools with no acquisition expenditure. Other record programs may provide some of the same capability, but the mapping capability appears unique.

Potential utility could be enhanced with the development of a school directory download capability and interfaces with mobile technologies that are now more commonly found in schools.

School COP has potential use for researchers in juvenile criminology. For example, researchers can use cleansed school-incident data to ascertain correlations between school-incident types and crime activity in a particular location. However, for such use to occur, privacy, information sharing, and data security policies and issues would need to be addressed.

### Potential as a Commercial Product

User feedback to the developer of School COP indicates that this tool is a very useful free product for school resource officers. The developer believes that a commercial package akin to School COP would require substantial additional investment, and schools would then need to purchase the package. As such, there are no current plans to commercialize School COP.

## Impact

NIJ's award to develop School COP resulted in a free, easy-to-use incident-mapping and database-creation tool that requires only minutes to download and use. The documentation takes only a short time to work through before the user can begin entering incident data. As a result of its user friendliness and a follow-on dissemination effort, School COP is used every day by a number of schools. Schools that desire a mapping capability can adapt School COP without expenditure of resources other than the time to enter the incidents in the database.

## Recommendations

Potential enhancements that might encourage more schools to use School COP include automatic download of information from school directories and developing some networking capability. A basic cost/benefit analysis should be conducted to determine whether a small limited investment to update School COP with such enhancements is feasible and cost-effective.

Any enhancement to School COP could be transferred to Facility Cop because Facility Cop was derived from School COP. (See "Facility Cop.")

School COP should continue to be featured in NIJ sources that publicize its geospatial software tools because School COP is a fully functional tool that runs on commonly available hardware, requires no additional tethering software, is well supported, and is being actively used by school resource officers. Including School COP in NIJ publicity on geospatial tools will increase School COP's visibility to other school officials looking for free incident database and mapping capabilities.

## Spatial Pattern Analysis for Investigative Decision Making Exploration and Response

### Technical Assessment

#### Function

SPIDER is a spatial statistics program for tactical crime analysis of linked crime-incident locations. SPIDER provides spatial and temporal diagnostic information, as well as commuter/marauder prediction,[12] geographic profiling, and next-event forecasting analysis. As such, SPIDER can be used to analyze and predict the possible next strike (next-event forecasting) or optimal location to begin looking for the offender (geographic profiling).

#### Software

SPIDER requires Microsoft MapPoint software version 2006 or later to geocode input data and display the output maps. The MapPoint website (Microsoft, undated) permits download for free trial and purchase (for approximately $300). SPIDER requires the user to supply crime-series data. This input file can be specified in several ways, including Excel files, .csv files, CrimeStat, or direct input into SPIDER.

Once any crimes are entered into the system, SPIDER automatically calculates the commuter and marauder diagnostics and displays them on an overview chart that is always visible on the main screen. The commuter and marauder numbers are static values that are the result of analysis of more than 110 solved crime series from more than 30 different jurisdictions. The values are median values from all the commuter offenders in those solved cases. The series values pertain to the series under consideration. Comparisons of the values from the

---

[12] Each offender is placed in one of two categories based on the spatial relationship between his or her crime sites and anchor points: commuter or marauder. Offenders whose anchor points are bounded by their crime locations are called marauders, and offenders whose crime sites are in a different physical area from their anchor points are called commuters. Determining the category into which a suspect falls is not always straightforward. SPIDER offers diagnostics to help the user choose the category into which to place the suspect. This diagnostic aid is the marauder/commuter prediction capability in SPIDER. The program advises the user to conduct next-event analysis if the suspect is a commuter and conduct geographic profile analysis if the suspect is categorized as a marauder.

series with the static values can help the analyst determine whether commuter/marauder analysis methods are most appropriate. Once the user has made a determination, he or she can select from a number of routines that will result in graphs or maps that display the optimal area in which to search for a suspect or the information regarding a probable next strike.

SPIDER-generated maps can be saved as Joint Photographic Experts Group (JPEG, with the file extension commonly being .jpg) or Polynomial Texture Mapping (PTM, with the file extension .ptm) files. SPIDER has a KML export function that allows the user to open the case data (profile, forecast, and crime locations) in the free Google Earth software. SPIDER also has an .shp export function that allows the user to open the case data in ArcGIS or another stand-alone GIS package. A toolbar offers a large number of manipulation options, such as creating territories, displaying the map on Bing Maps, and sending the map as a text message to a mobile phone. Right-clicking on the map is another way to bring up some of these options.

Run times were short on a three-year-old PC laptop. The graphs appeared nearly instantaneously in pop-up windows. The color-coded maps took a couple of minutes to display. A rose color indicates the (rectangular) areas of highest probability, orange indicates the next-highest, yellow next, blue next, and green the lowest. Once the user is familiar with this color scheme, the maps are intuitive to interpret.

### Hardware
SPIDER runs on Windows 2000 or more-recent Windows systems.

### Data
The input data must contain a label or identifier, location, date, and time for each crime. The user's manual details the procedures for importing the input file using the various vehicles and the correct format for each type of input file. Location data can be supplied as an address, and SPIDER will determine the latitude/longitude for the address. SPIDER allows the user to edit the input data, and all input files are automatically geocoded with MapPoint. Crime-series input files can be saved for subsequent SPIDER runs.

### User Preparations

SPIDER is designed to be used by experienced crime analysts. The three-day training course or careful review of the training material is required to use the tool. College-level statistics is required to understand the underlying theory. Familiarity with Excel and MapPoint is helpful.

### Support

SPIDER support material includes a workbook, a three-day training course, and PowerPoint presentations for the three-day training course. Separate versions of the support material are available for Windows and Mac OS X. The workbook includes background material on spatial analysis, a guide to using SPIDER, and material to help with selection of routines and interpretation of the results. The resulting maps and charts are intuitive but require crime-analysis background to interpret. The training course will be offered periodically by the IACA using an updated curriculum and workbooks.

SPIDER and all of its supporting documentation are available at Paulsen (undated).

## Operational Assessment

### Current Utility

SPIDER provides spatial and temporal diagnostic information, as well as commuter and marauder prediction, geographic profiling, and next-event forecasting analysis. It can be used to quickly produce maps and charts regarding a crime series. A number of existing programs, such as CrimeStat, Rigel Analyst, and Dragnet, can perform the same functions. Like CrimeStat (see above), SPIDER is free and quick. It uses a time-weighted kernel density interpolation method for next-event forecasting and center-of-minimum-distance approach for geographic profiling that other programs do not. Studies have shown these approaches to be at least as accurate as or more accurate than other methods (Paulsen, 2005, 2006; Paulsen, Bair, and Helms, 2010). Hence SPIDER offers users an alternative or additional capability to perform next-event forecasting and geographic profiling. In addition, users have found the commuter and marauder diagnostic charts that are always displayed to be very useful, and these are unique to SPIDER.

SPIDER is a product with a dissemination plan.

### Potential Enhancements and Limitations

The primary limitation to SPIDER is that the user must determine whether the crimes being considered were committed by the same person, and this is difficult to determine. Although SPIDER provides some basic guidance on this topic, some capability to identify series patterns or link to such a capability would be an enhancement to SPIDER. There are potential enhancements of an administrative nature that do not affect SPIDER's functionality but might help the user. One is that the axes in some of the output plots are not labeled, so an analyst has to remember what output graph was selected and, if more than one is displayed, which represents what. Another is that labels on some output files appear to be selected for the crime analysts (e.g., average days between crimes), while others appear to be selected for mathematicians (e.g., area of convex hull, area of a standard deviational ellipse). Only experienced criminologists with college-level statistics knowledge would know how to interpret the area of a convex hull or the area of a standard deviational ellipse for crime analysis.

### Potential Utility

Primary users of SPIDER are crime analysts. Once training is complete, SPIDER offers a relatively quick, easy-to-use, and comprehensive tool to help users analyze crime series. Built-in or complementary automated capabilities to help crime analysts identify patterns and determine whether crimes should be associated with a single individual would make SPIDER an even more useful tool.

Researchers developing tools and capabilities for law enforcement may find SPIDER useful to make comparisons in approaches to address geographic profiling and next-event forecasting.

### Potential as a Commercial Product

SPIDER is a free to all users, and there are no plans to turn it into a commercial product.

## Impact

SPIDER offers the law enforcement community a powerful and comprehensive tool to help analyze crime series. Users have stated that it has improved their efficiency in analyzing crime series.

## Recommendations

SPIDER is a popular tool. Plans are already in place to update the training material for this tool. SPIDER should continue to be featured in NIJ sources that publicize its geospatial software tools because the program is a fully functional, well-supported tool that can help the law enforcement community analyze crime.

## Urban Crime Simulator

### Technical Assessment

#### Function

UCS allows a user to use his or her own data to simulate or estimate changes in crime rates in a city, at neighborhood level of his or her choice.

#### Software

This review is based on developer-provided information because no users of UCS could be found and the software lacks the technical maturity required for the study team to independently evaluate the tool.

The current version of UCS is tethered to ArcGIS Engine 9.2 and is incompatible with more-recent versions of ArcGIS Engine.

#### Hardware

UCS runs only on Windows XP. A minimum processor speed of 1 GHz is required. In addition, a minimum of 1 GB of RAM and 1 GB of hard disk capacity are required to install and run. A 1 MB graphics board and display with minimum 800 × 600 resolution is required.

### Data

User-provided data must be in .shp format. The user must provide crime data sets for the communities.

### User Preparations

The developer states that a high school education plus 30 minutes of training is sufficient to use UCS.

### Support

The developer states that a user's guide is available.

UCS is available at Urban Operations Research (undated). The website includes background literature, an installation guide, and descriptions of the UCS algorithms.

## Operational Assessment

### Current Utility

The current version of UCS is tethered to ArcGIS Engine 9.2 and runs only on Windows XP computers. The software cannot be used without ArcGIS Engine 9.2. The current version of ArcGIS Engine is 10.1, and ArcGIS Engine is not backward compatible, so even if a current ArcGIS Engine license is secured for $1,500, UCS will still not run without installing ArcGIS Engine 9.2. These conditions make the tool less attractive to practitioners. No users of UCS could be found. Because the tool lacks the technical maturity to be evaluated by the study team, the team observed no current utility to law enforcement practitioners.

### Potential Enhancements and Limitations

The primary limitation to UCS is its tethering to ArcGIS Engine 9.2 and compatibility to a single version of Windows. No current users could be found, and there are not likely to be any users until UCS is ported to independently executable software that does not rely on ArcGIS Engine and is compatible with current versions of Windows.

### Potential Utility

There is no potential utility for UCS unless the tool is freed from its tie to ArcGIS Engine 9.2 and its reliance on Windows XP is extended to include later versions of Windows.

### Potential as a Commercial Product

The developer believes that there are no barriers to commercialize UCS, but there are no plans to pursue commercialization.

## Impact

UCS has had no impact on the law enforcement community to date because of a lack of users. Criminology researchers might find descriptions of the algorithms useful in their explorations of how to extend applications of spatial statistical methods to crime analysis.

## Recommendations

We recommend that NIJ perform a basic cost/benefit analysis to determine whether a small additional investment can transform the current version of UCS to software independent of ArcGIS Engine and compatible with current versions of Windows. We make this recommendation because the sunk cost for developing UCS has so far resulted in no benefit for the law enforcement community. Additionally, there appeared to be much potential interest in the functionality provided by UCS when it was first being developed. For example, at the October 2012 NIJ Geospatial Technology Working Group meeting, an attendee stated that he would like to use UCS to view trends associated with calls for service (U.S. Department of Justice [DOJ], 2010). NIJ might therefore explore whether additional investment to remove the tool's dependence on ArcGIS Engine 9.2 and Windows XP could result in some benefit to the law enforcement community.

# CHAPTER FOUR

# Overall Evaluations, Findings, and Recommendations

## Overall Evaluations from a Holistic Perspective

Assessments and evaluations of the individual tools were presented in Chapter Three. In this chapter, we synthesize what we have learned and observed to present a holistic view of the tools. This synthesis offers a high-level view of the impact and benefits to the law enforcement community from recent NIJ geospatial software tool awards. A summary view of the synthesis is presented first. Next, we discuss our overall findings. Finally, we present the recommendations that stem from the findings.

Table 4.1 shows a summary view of the various tools reviewed for this study. The first column in Table 4.1 shows the name of the tool. The second column contains a short description of the function of the tool. The third column indicates the status of each tool. The term *fully functional* in the third column (and throughout this report) means that the tool performs its intended function as evidenced by our independent assessment, user feedback, and developer demonstrations. The fourth column summarizes actions NIJ can take to improve the current version of each tool.

As Table 4.1 shows, CrimeStat and SPIDER are fully functional tools with excellent support material. Both require in-depth familiarity with the training material to use. SPIDER requires MapPoint ($300), and CrimeStat requires a separate GIS. School COP and its derivative, Facility Cop, are fully functional tools that are very easy to use. Geographic Profiler is a fully functional tool with excellent support material. Its main drawback is its long run times. In the cases

**Table 4.1**
**Summary View of Observations**

| Geospatial Tool | Function | Action to Improve |
|---|---|---|
| ArcGIS 10.2 PySAL Tool | Tool provides basic spatial regression functionality (spatial lag and spatial error model) and the ability to convert and transform spatial weights matrices within the widely-used ArcGIS | In progress |
| CAST | Allows user to analyze and visualize crimes in space-time frameworks using PySAL functionality | In progress |
| CrimeStat | Spatial statistics program for the analysis of crime-incident locations | Planned release of next version may address user-identified issues. |
| Facility Cop | Prison-incident database creation, mapping, and report generation | Update of School COP can be exploited to update Facility Cop |
| GeoDaNet | Identifies clusters of crimes on networks and calculates distances based on street distance rather than straight-line distance. | In progress |
| GeoDaSpace | Generates views of crimes as function of environmental design characteristics and other variables | In progress |
| Geographic Profiler | Generates probable location of serial offender's anchor point based on locations of offender's previous crimes | Unclear run times can be significantly decreased with software modifications. As computing power of computers increase, prototype run times will decrease. |
| Mobile Semi-Automated 3-D | Provides 3-D location and movement information for first responders | Unclear |

**Table 4.1—Continued**

| Geospatial Tool | Function | Action to Improve |
|---|---|---|
| Near Repeat Calculator | Generates estimates of increased probability crime will take place within distance and time of recent crime | Additional investment for GPS-coordinate compatibility and address data input burdens |
| OpenGeoDa | NIJ-funded functionality is spatial data analysis across time | Plan in place, non-NIJ sponsors |
| PySAL | Python-based library of spatial-analysis functions. NIJ-funded algorithms include local cluster detection for polygons, cluster statistics for crimes on streets, computation of street distances between points and crime locations, spatial regression modeling, spatial diagnostic tests for probit models. | In progress |
| School COP | School-incident database creation, mapping, and report generation | Additional investment to update |
| SPIDER | Spatial statistics program for the tactical crime analysis of linked crime-incident locations | Plan in place |
| UCS | Allows users to use their own data to estimate changes in crime rates in their city, at neighborhood level | Additional investment to remove dependence on ArcGIS Engine 9.2 and Windows XP |

NOTE: Shading indicates a tool that was not evaluated because tool was not available or lacked technical maturity to perform an evaluation.

in which long run times are immaterial, Geographic Profiler can be another valuable tool in a crime analyst's tool kit. PySAL is a library of geospatial statistical routines for tool developers. Its installation process is being simplified. OpenGeoDa is a fully functional tool. Support materials are being updated, but the large user base of previous versions of OpenGeoDa are not likely to require updated support material to use the latest version of this tool. GeoDaSpace, GeoDaNet, and the ArcGIS 10.2 PySAL Tool are fully functional tools that are not yet in final release. Support materials are in progress for GeoDaSpace and the ArcGIS 10.2 PySAL Tool. An ArcGIS desktop license is required for the ArcGIS 10.2 PySAL Tool. CAST had not yet been released during the time frame of this study, but the pre-alpha demonstration version suggests an impressive product. Support material is being developed for CAST. UCS was not evaluated for this study because of the tool's technical immaturity (UCS is tethered to ArcGIS Engine 9.2 and runs only on Windows XP, both of which are outdated, and these properties essentially render the tool inaccessible). Mobile Semi-Automated 3-D was not evaluated because it was not made available for this study. We were unable to confirm whether access to Mobile Semi-Automated 3-D is feasible.

CrimeStat, SPIDER, PySAL, GeoDaSpace, GeoDaNet, the ArcGIS 10.2 PySAL Tool, CAST, and OpenGeoDa all have plans in place or are in the process of being improved. Geographic Profiler can be improved with a decrease in its long run times, but it is unclear whether significant decreases can be achieved with software modifications alone. The complexity of the algorithms inherent in Geographic Profiler may just require a high level of computing power. In any case, its run times should decrease as computers become faster. School COP, the Near Repeat Calculator, and UCS may all benefit from a cost/benefit analysis to determine whether small additional investments by NIJ can bring other benefits to the law enforcement community. A cost/benefit analysis for School COP should focus on updating the tool to enable automatic download of school directories. Any improvement to School COP is transferable to Facility Cop. A cost/benefit analysis of the Near Repeat Calculator should focus on making the tool compatible with GPS coordinates. Use of GPS has grown over recent years, and such devices are now commonly used to generate location coordinates. The Near Repeat Calculator may therefore be easier for law enforcement to use if it can be modified for compatibility with GPS coordinates. Cost/benefit analysis of UCS should focus on removing this tool's tethering to outdated ArcGIS Engine 9.2 and Windows XP, thus enabling access. Finally, it is unclear what action would enable access to Mobile Semi-Automated 3-D.

## Findings and Recommendations

In this section, we take a holistic view of the geospatial software task. From this higher-level perspective, findings emerge that suggest ways in which NIJ can maximize benefits that future geospatial tool developments have for the law enforcement community. In the discussions in this section, we present our findings and recommendations that stem from the findings.

### Post–Solicitation Policy Inconsistencies and Gaps

There are many models that identify the structure and processes inherent in creating a software product, such as geospatial software tools. Examples include the waterfall model (Royce, 1970), the spiral model (Boehm, 1986), the agile model (Abrahamsson et al., 2002), the rapid application development (RAD) model (Whitten, Bentley, and Dittman, 2003), the Carnegie Mellon University (CMU) Software Engineering Institute (SEI) life-cycle model (Linger et al., 2002), and the international standard for software development issued jointly by the International Organization for Standardization (ISO) and the International Electrotechnical Commission (IEC) called *Systems and Software Engineering: Software Life Cycle Processes* (ISO/IEC 12207:2008) (ISO/IEC, 2008). All of these models and ISO/IEC 12207:2008 recognize that, for software development to provide intended functionality to its target audience, all of the development phases must be properly executed. DOJ makes this same recognition in its Systems Development Life Cycle framework for technology system development. The DOJ framework shows ten phases that must be executed for development of software, such as geospatial software tools: initiation, system concept development, planning, requirement analysis, design, development, integration and test, implementation, operations and maintenance, and disposition. This means that DOJ policy assigns roles and responsibilities to DOJ officials to execute the phases. Table 4.2 shows the ten phases of the DOJ framework and the mapping of those phases to other commonly known software life-cycle models.[1]

Evaluation of NIJ-funded developments of geospatial software tools reveals potential policy gaps and inconsistencies in the assignment and execution of roles and responsibilities associated with the development, integration and test, implementation, and operations and maintenance phases of the DOJ framework. For each of the geospatial tools evaluated, NIJ successfully executed the first four phases of the life cycle, from effectively using technology working groups to identify law enforcement needs through formulating solicitations and selecting awardees with creative and theoretically solid approaches to extend the use of spatial analysis to the law enforcement community. The apparent inconsistencies and gaps occur in the phases that follow solicitation. These are discussed below.

### Award Clauses

The first gap surfaces at the award phase, in which it appears that NIJ does not always include a software delivery clause along with a final report delivery provision as terms of the award. Although each award must be tailored to the specific development, NIJ could benefit from always ensuring that the funded tool is delivered or made accessible to NIJ at some point. We note that NIJ does not always provide all of the funds necessary to develop a functional tool, so delivery of software at the conclusion of NIJ funding might not always be practical. Nonetheless, even in complicated instances, in which multiple funding sources are involved or other unusual circumstances are present, NIJ could benefit from including a viable way for it to receive or access a version of the funded product, functional or not, at some point, even if deliv-

---

[1]   See the appendix for brief descriptions of ISO/IEC 12207:2008 and the waterfall, spiral, agile, and RAD models.

**Table 4.2**
**Mapping of the U.S. Department of Justice Systems Development Life Cycle Framework to ISO/IEC 12207:2008 and Other Software Life-Cycle Models**

| DOJ | ISO/IEC | Waterfall | Spiral | Agile | RAD | CMU SEI |
|---|---|---|---|---|---|---|
| Initiation | Acquisition | System requirements / Software requirements | Requirements | Concept creation | Requirements planning | Mission definition |
| System concept development | | | | Requirements analysis | | Concept of operations |
| Planning | Supply | Analysis | Design | Design | Design | Project planning |
| Requirements analysis | Development | Program design | Code / Integration / Test | Coding / Testing | Construction | Requirements definition |
| Design | | | | | | System specification |
| | | | | | | System architecture |
| | | Coding | | | | System design |
| Development | | | | | | System implementation |
| Integration and test | | Testing | | | | System test |
| Implementation | | | Implementation / Release | | | |
| Operations and maintenance | Operations / Maintenance | Operations | | Release | Cutover | System evolution |
| Disposition | Destruction | | | | | |

ery must occur after the delivery of a final report. Examples include the six tools (PySAL, GeoDaSpace, GeoDaNet, the ArcGIS 10.2 PySAL Tool, CAST, and OpenGeoDa) that ASU developed or is developing using NIJ funds as seed funding. NIJ did not include a software delivery clause in its contract with ASU, but NIJ will receive more tool capabilities than it funded because ASU is harnessing the synergistic benefits of multiple funding sources and is delivering spatial statistical tools for the law enforcement community and other communities. A simpler case is School COP. NIJ funded the development of School COP, the award included the School COP executable as a deliverable, and there were no compliance issues. Mobile Semi-Automated 3-D development is less clear. No software was delivered with the final report, and, for the duration of this study, the tool was inaccessible for evaluation.[2] We recommend that NIJ always include a tool-delivery clause unless it is clear that absence of an end product is an acceptable end state of the development.

In addition, our evaluation has shown that documentation of the geospatial software tool can range from detailed (in which the documentation supplies many explanations about how the tool functions and how the tool might be used) to sparse (in which the documentation explains only how to access, install, and execute the tool). Tool documentation cannot be expected to be in final form for those tools that are in early test release stages, and NIJ would need to recognize such situations in its award negotiations. Tool developments that will result in final release versions, however, should always be accompanied by a user's manual or some other form of tool training. We recommend that NIJ include a clause in future awards for geospatial tool developments that requires the developer to deliver and provide access to tool documentation.

### Oversight

The second gap appears at the design phase. Although NIJ has shown a remarkable ability to select a spectrum of tool capabilities and qualified

---

[2]   NIJ received the source code for Mobile Semi-Automated 3-D in the first quarter of 2013, after the conclusion of the evaluation phase of this study.

developers with novel approaches, some additional oversight during the design process might help NIJ maximize the tools' benefits to the law enforcement community. For example, decisions on technical approach can result in unintentionally limiting the potential tool user base. A specific instance is the decision to tether UCS to ArcGIS Engine. This decision resulted in a tool that requires the user to spend significant up-front funds to buy ArcGIS Engine. The fact that ArcGIS Engine is not backward compatible significantly decreased the accessibility of UCS. In addition, the tool runs only on Windows XP systems. A second specific example is the decision during the design of the Near Repeat Calculator that resulted in incompatibility with GPS coordinates. Use of GPS coordinates has been increasing for years, and the intricacies of converting from GPS to rectilinear coordinates were also well known during the design phase of this tool. GPS incompatibility makes the tool less attractive to the law enforcement community. Although these particular decisions may have been due to resource constraints or the increased complexities of developing a new, unique capability and hence well justified, full understanding of the consequences by the developer and NIJ before proceeding could prove highly valuable. We recommend that an informal review process be considered to ensure full understanding of the consequences of major technical approach decisions on the tool utility.

### Roles and Responsibilities

The third apparent policy gap surfaces at the tool implementation juncture that follows development. As shown in Figure 4.1, no NIJ or other DOJ office appears to have taken on the role of tool dissemination and assumed the responsibilities inherent in operations and maintenance of the NIJ-funded geospatial tools. We recommend an examination of NIJ policy to clarify specification of roles and responsibilities to execute effective tool implementation, operations, and maintenance. Policies permitting, we encourage NIJ to stay involved through the sustainment phases to ensure continuity in tool development. If there is a gap in policies, we recommend expanding roles and responsibilities of NIJ officials to take charge throughout the life cycle to enable follow-through and increase ties to the user community.

**Figure 4.1**
**U.S. Department of Justice System Development Life Cycle**

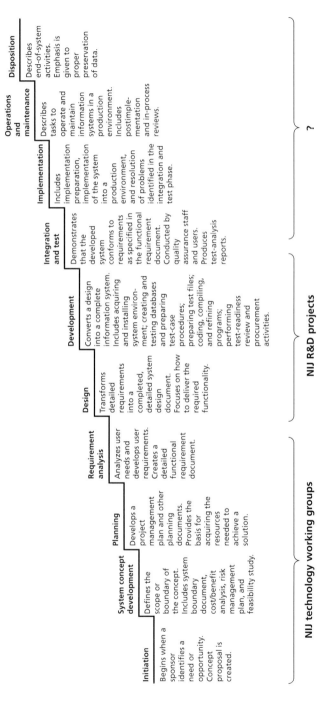

SOURCE: U.S. Department of Justice, 2003.

RAND RR418-4.1

**Tool-Dissemination Plans**

The utility of geospatial software tools could potentially be enhanced with development of a dissemination plan specific to each tool. Development of a dissemination plan was not included as a requirement for any of the geospatial software development awards examined in this evaluation. Lack of a basic dissemination plan inhibits the establishment of a tool user base. A basic dissemination plan would identify an appropriate marketing scheme that identifies the potential audience and notifies potential users in the law enforcement community of tool deployment. Such a basic plan would also address operations and maintenance issues, such as establishment of a contact for tool-related questions, error reporting, and suggestions; a tool-update strategy; and tool-retirement criteria. School COP provides an example of the power of a dissemination plan. School COP successfully pursued a postdevelopment contract with COPS to essentially make the tool's target audience aware of the tool's existence and capabilities—in short, the follow-on contract included development and implementation of a tool-dissemination plan. That follow-up contract allowed the School COP developers to enhance the accessibility of the tool and monitor its adoption. The result is a tool with outstanding support material and wide appeal and awareness that is used every day by many schools. We recommend that all future geospatial tool-development contracts include a clause for development of a basic tool-dissemination plan. Implementation of the plan would be monitored by those responsible for tool implementation (see potential policy gaps illustrated in Figure 4.1).

**Go-To Sources for Tool Notification**

Our conversations with tool users and developers revealed that there is no established source (e.g., website, office, publication, app) for the law enforcement community to learn about the existence of geospatial software tools developed with NIJ funding and experiment with the tools. In some cases, potential users were surprised to find that there was an NIJ-funded geospatial tool available free of charge that provided capabilities that law enforcement agencies were currently buying from commercial sources. Although no comparisons of actual capabilities were made between the NIJ tool and the commercial tools, these comments reveal that some potential users are simply not aware of NIJ-funded tools and do not know where to find out about them. We recommend the establishment of one or more sources from which potential users are notified of NIJ-funded developments. Routine updates of such sources could potentially increase the user base for the tools.

## Process for Postdelivery Modifications

NIJ funding of modifications to address shortfalls or beneficial improvements in delivered geospatial software tools can result in a high return on investment in terms of higher tool adoption and more routine users. In some cases, there are known technical shortfalls with a tool, or user feedback points to modifications that would greatly enhance the utility of the tools and foster closer ties to the operational community. Such ties can lead to more-focused development of future research and development efforts. Examples include enabling a function to import a school directory in School COP to reduce the data-entry burden that potential users have cited as a drawback and reducing the current long run times of Geographic Profiler that make the tool impractical in some user environments. NIJ has already invested in the successful development of all tools evaluated—the NIJ funds invested to develop a tool are sunk costs at tool delivery. A basic cost/benefit analysis can determine whether a small additional investment by NIJ can mitigate a user issue and make a tool more attractive to potential users. We recommend that, when user issues arise, NIJ conduct a basic cost/benefit analysis to determine whether a small additional investment would substantially increase the utility of each tool. Investing an additional nominal sum may yield substantial benefit in the cases in which the potential benefit is found to far outweigh the additional investment.

## Tool Interoperability

Our conversations with tool users and tool developers revealed that tool adoption is influenced by the tool's interoperability and networking capabilities. Some of the NIJ-funded tool developments resulted in stand-alone tools that are installed on a single computer and do not have networking capabilities. Others are not interoperable with other tools already in use by a potential user. These characteristics can limit the tool's utility for a particular user and hence lead to non-adoption of the tool, even though the capability may be desired. For example, several users commented that, even though they had the NIJ-funded tools, they did not use them routinely because using them meant opening another application, preparing the input data files, running the tool, and then trying to compare the results with the output from the tools routinely employed. Although none of these steps is difficult, some users view them as burdensome and detrimental to keeping one's train of thought during an active analysis. Ideally, users would have the NIJ tools be extensions that use a single common input database in which the user need only specify the data elements to include for a particular tool application and tools could be triggered with a single click. A single common database for a suite of tools is feasible but may require NIJ to take the lead to establish guidelines or standards. We recommend that NIJ examine this issue further.

From the developers' perspective, tool adoption is an issue. Many systems used by law enforcement agencies are not inherently interoperable. Tools often have to be tailored to individual law enforcement agencies. The resource expenditures to effect such tailoring can be costly both in funds and time, and NIJ contracts do not include allowances for adoption. We recommend that NIJ consider this issue along with the implementation and tool-dissemination issues discussed above.

Information sharing and interoperability of law enforcement information technology are emerging issues that could benefit from additional attention from NIJ. For example, one agency estimated that making a tool interoperable to share information between two information technology systems required three months to develop, test, and implement transition code after successful negotiation of multiple contracts. The development of national databases, such as the Federal Bureau of Investigation (FBI) facial recognition database, will increase the demand for information sharing among national, state, and local law enforcement agencies. We recommend that NIJ start to identify the alternative approaches to achieving interoperable systems that will permit the information sharing that law enforcement will increasingly demand.

## Closing Remarks

Our geospatial tool evaluation shows that, in 12 out of 14 cases, NIJ received fully functional geospatial tools. In addition, NIJ selected a spectrum of qualified developers with novel approaches to extend the use of geospatial tools to the law enforcement community. Our exchanges with developers and users indicate a few areas in which NIJ can take actions to ensure that future geospatial tool developments provide maximal benefits to the law enforcement community. These include addressing several apparent policy gaps and inconsistencies, including ensuring that policies assign NIJ or Department of Justice officials roles and responsibilities for the latter phases of software development, including integration and test, implementation, operations and maintenance, and disposition; developing tool-dissemination plans; establishing a go-to source for tool-deployment notifications; establishing a process and modest funding to address postdevelopment tool shortfalls; and taking the lead to address emerging interoperability and information sharing issues. Acting on these recommendations should enhance NIJ's ability to consistently deliver maximal benefits to the law enforcement community from future geospatial tool developments.

# ISO/IEC 12207:2008 and Software Life-Cycle Models

This appendix provides brief descriptions of the software life-cycle standard called ISO/IEC 12207:2008 and the waterfall, spiral, agile, and RAD software life-cycle models.

The waterfall model originated from the manufacturing and construction industries but has been applied to software development for decades (Royce, 1970). The waterfall model identifies system requirements, software requirements, analysis, program design, coding, testing, and operations as the primary processes. The spiral model emphasizes risk analysis and the iterative nature of software development (Boehm, 1986). The processes in the spiral model are requirements, design, code, integration, test, implementation, and release. The agile model builds in feedback as a critical component of the iterative nature of software development (Abrahamsson et al., 2002). The processes in the agile model are concept creation, requirement analysis, design, coding, testing, and release. The RAD model minimizes planning and emphasizes prototype development (Whitten, Bentley, and Dittman, 2003). The processes included in the RAD model are requirement planning, design, construction, and cutover. The CMU SEI model is a generic model that can be adapted to emphasize a variety of software characteristics, such as systems that are highly survivable (Linger et al., 2002). The processes included in the CMU SEI model are mission definition, concept of operations, project planning, requirement definition, system specification, system architecture, system design, system implementation, system test, and system evolution.

Although the models use different terminology and different definitions of the same terminology, all recognize that there are fundamental processes underlying every software development. In an effort to facilitate communications among software users, suppliers, developers, maintainers, operators, managers, technicians, and any other entities that may be involved in the definition, acquisition, control, use, and improvement of software, ISO and the IEC jointly published an international standard for software development. The latest version of this standard is ISO/IEC 12207:2008, *Systems and Software Engineering: Software Life Cycle Processes*. It establishes an internationally recognized common structure for software life-cycle processes that is used by public and private sectors worldwide. The ISO/IEC 12207:2008 common structure identifies six core processes involved in creating a software product. These are acquisition, supply, development, operation, maintenance, and destruction. Acquisition includes activities from need determination to system requirement definition, proposal solicitation and evaluation, contract negotiations and award, acceptance testing, and configuration management of deliverables. The majority of activities performed by NIJ for geospatial tool developments fall into the ISO/IEC core acquisition process. *Supply* is the ISO/IEC term for project management planning and oversight. Development includes software design, creation, and testing. Development activities for NIJ-funded geospatial software tools are performed by the awardee. Operations and maintenance activities occur simultaneously and are user based. These activities assist the user in working with the software product and addressing any enhancements, changes, additions, and support issues. Destruction consists of activities to retire or end support of a software product.

ISO/IEC 12207:2008 incorporates two basic principles: modularity and responsibility. Modularity allows entities to tailor the standard to their software projects, and responsibility establishes accountability to facilitate passing control of software development among stakeholders throughout the software life cycle. Table A.1 compares ISO/IEC 12207:2008 and the five other models.

**Table A.1**
**Comparison of Software Development Life-Cycle Models**

| ISO/IEC 12207:2008 | Waterfall | Spiral | Agile | RAD | CMU SEI |
|---|---|---|---|---|---|
| Acquisition | System requirements / Software requirements | Requirements | Concept creation / Requirements analysis | Requirements planning | Mission definition / Concept of operations |
| Supply | Analysis | Design | Design | Design | Project planning |
| Development | Program design | Code / Integration / Test | Coding / Testing | Construction | Requirements definition |
| | | | | | System specification |
| | | | | | System architecture |
| | | | | | System design |
| | Coding | | | | System implementation |
| | Testing | | | | System test |
| Operations | Operations | Implementation / Release | Release | Cutover | System evolution |
| Maintenance | | | | | |
| Destruction | | | | | |

# Bibliography

Abrahamsson, Pekka, Outi Salo, Jussi Ronkainen, and Juhani Warsta, *Agile Software Development Methods: Review and Analysis*, Espoo: VTT Electronics, Publication 478, 2002. As of January 23, 2014:
http://www.vtt.fi/inf/pdf/publications/2002/P478.pdf

Anselin, Luc, *GeoDa™ 0.9 User's Guide*, Center for Spatially Integrated Social Science, revised June 15, 2003. As of January 23, 2014:
https://geodacenter.org/downloads/pdfs/geoda093.pdf

———, *GeoDa™ 0.9.5-i Release Notes*, Center for Spatially Integrated Social Science, revised January 20, 2004. As of January 23, 2014:
https://geodacenter.org/downloads/pdfs/geoda095i.pdf

———, *Exploring Spatial Data with GeoDa™: A Workbook*, Center for Spatially Integrated Social Science, revised March 6, 2005. As of January 23, 2014:
https://geodacenter.asu.edu/system/files/geodaworkbook.pdf

———, *Linking and Brushing*, briefing, Chicago, Ill., July 25–27, 2012a. As of January 23, 2014:
http://moodle.geodapress.com/mod/resource/view.php?id=685

———, *Quick Tour of OpenGeoda*, briefing, Chicago, Ill., July 25–27, 2012b. As of January 23, 2014:
http://moodle.geodapress.com/mod/resource/view.php?id=683

———, *Space-Time Mapping*, briefing, Chicago, Ill., July 25–27, 2012c. As of January 23, 2014:
http://moodle.geodapress.com/mod/resource/view.php?id=684

Applied Geography, Kent State University, "Welcome!" undated. As of January 23, 2014:
http://gis.kent.edu/urbancrimesimulator/

Boehm, B., "A Spiral Model of Software Development and Enhancement," *ACM SIGSOFT Software Engineering Notes*, Vol. 11, No. 4, August 1986, pp. 14–24.

Brown, A. W., and K. C. Wallnau, "A Framework for Evaluating Software Technology," *IEEE Software*, Vol. 13, No. 5, September 1996, pp. 39–49.

Charlotte Visualization Center, "Project Abstract," undated. As of January 23, 2014:
http://viscenter.uncc.edu/research/mobile-system-urban-emergency-response

Esri, "Pricing," undated, referenced April 27, 2013. As of January 23, 2014:
http://www.esri.com/software/arcgis/arcgis-for-desktop/pricing

Finn, Peter, Meg Townsend, Michael Shively, and Tom Rich, *A Guide to Developing, Maintaining, and Succeeding with Your School Resource Officer Program*, Washington, D.C.: U.S. Department of Justice, Office of Community Oriented Policing Services, June 2005. As of January 23, 2014:
http://www.cops.usdoj.gov/Publications/sroguidelines.pdf

GeoDa Center for Geospatial Analysis and Computation, "ArcGIS 10.2 PySAL Tool," undated (a). As of January 23, 2014:
https://geodacenter.asu.edu/arc_pysal

———, "Crime Analytics for Space-Time (CAST)," undated (b). As of January 23, 2014:
https://geodacenter.asu.edu/cast

———, "Download GeoDa," undated (c). As of January 23, 2014:
https://geodacenter.asu.edu/software/downloads

———, "GeoDaNet Alpha Download," undated (d). As of February 16, 2014:
https://geodacenter.asu.edu/downloads/software/gnet

———, "GeoDaSpace Alpha Downloads," undated (e). As of February 16, 2014:
https://geodacenter.asu.edu/software/downloads/geodaspace

———, "Open GeoDa," undated (f). As of January 23, 2014:
https://geodacenter.asu.edu/ogeoda

———, "PySAL: Open Source Python Library for Spatial Analytical Functions," undated (g). As of January 23, 2014:
https://geodacenter.asu.edu/pysal

———, "GeoDa Center Releases GeoDaSpace Alpha," January 16, 2012. As of January 23, 2014:
https://geodacenter.asu.edu/geodaspace_alpha

International Organization for Standardization/International Electrotechnical Commission, *Systems and Software Engineering: Software Life Cycle Processes*, ISO/IEC 12207:2008, 2008.

Inter-University Consortium for Political and Social Research, "*CrimeStat*® III," undated (a). As of January 24, 2014:
http://www.icpsr.umich.edu/CrimeStat/

————, "Download *CrimeStat*," undated (b). As of January 24, 2014:
http://www.icpsr.umich.edu/CrimeStat/download.html

ISO/IEC—*See* International Organization for Standardization/International Electrotechnical Commission.

Jackson, Mike, Steve Crouch, and Rob Baxter, "Software Evaluation Guide," Edinburgh: Software Sustainability Institute, last updated August 19, 2013. As of January 23, 2014:
http://www.software.ac.uk/software-evaluation-guide

Johnson, Shane D., Wim Bernasco, Kate J. Bowers, Henk Elffers, Jerry Ratcliffe, George Rengert, and Michael Townsley, "Space-Time Patterns of Risk: A Cross National Assessment of Residential Burglary Victimization," *Journal of Quantitative Criminology*, Vol. 23, No. 3, September 2007, pp. 201–219.

Lazaris, Louis, "Release Histories for All Major Browsers," *Impressive Webs*, March 12, 2012. As of January 23, 2013:
http://www.impressivewebs.com/release-history-major-browsers/

Levine, Ned, *CrimeStat: A Spatial Statistics Program for the Analysis of Crime Incident Locations*, version 1.0, Houston, Texas: Ned Levine and Associates, August 1999.

————, *CrimeStat, Version 1.1 Update Release Notes*, Houston, Texas: Ned Levine and Associates, July 2000.

————, *CrimeStat: A Spatial Statistics Program for the Analysis of Crime Incident Locations*, version 2.0, Houston, Texas: Ned Levine and Associates, May 2002. As of January 23, 2014:
http://www.icpsr.umich.edu/CrimeStat/files/CrimeStat-2.0.zip

————, *CrimeStat: A Spatial Statistics Program for the Analysis of Crime Incident Locations*, version 3.0, Houston, Texas: Ned Levine and Associates, March 2005. As of January 23, 2014:
http://www.icpsr.umich.edu/CrimeStat/files/CrimeStat-3.0.zip

————, *CrimeStat Version 3.1 Update Notes*, Houston, Texas: Ned Levine and Associates, March 2007. As of January 23, 2014:
http://www.icpsr.umich.edu/CrimeStat/files/CrimeStat-3.1.zip

————, *CrimeStat Version 3.2a Update Notes*, Houston, Texas: Ned Levine and Associates, October 2009. As of January 23, 2014:
http://www.icpsr.umich.edu/CrimeStat/files/CrimeStat-3.2a.zip

————, *CrimeStat: A Spatial Statistics Program for the Analysis of Crime Incident Locations*, version 3.3, Houston, Texas: Ned Levine and Associates, July 2010a. As of January 23, 2014:
http://www.icpsr.umich.edu/CrimeStat/

———, *CrimeStat Version 3.3 Update Notes*, Part I: *Fixes Getis-Ord G Bayesian Journey-to-Crime*, Houston, Texas: Ned Levine and Associates, July 2010. As of January 23, 2014:
http://www.icpsr.umich.edu/CrimeStat/files/CrimeStat3.3updatenotesPartI.pdf

Levine, Ned, Dominique Lord, Byung-Jung Park, *CrimeStat Version 3.3 Update Notes*, Part 2: *Regression Modeling*, Houston, Texas: Ned Levine and Associates, July 2010. As of January 23, 2014:
http://www.icpsr.umich.edu/CrimeStat/files/CrimeStat3.3updatenotesPartII.pdf

Linger, Richard C., Howard F. Lipson, John McHugh, Nancy R. Mead, and Carol A. Sledge, *Life-Cycle Models for Survivable Systems*, Pittsburgh, Pa.: Software Engineering Institute, CMU/SEI-2002-TR-026, October 2002. As of January 23, 2014:
http://resources.sei.cmu.edu/library/asset-view.cfm?assetID=6201

Microsoft, "Microsoft® MapPoint®," undated. As of January 23, 2014:
http://www.microsoft.com/mappoint/en-us/home.aspx

Ned Levine and Associates, "CrimeStat® III Version 3.0, A Spatial Statistics Program for the Analysis of Crime Incident Locations," Houston, Texas, November 2004. As of January 23, 2014:
http://www.icpsr.umich.edu/CrimeStat/files/CrimeStatTableofContents.pdf

O'Leary, Mike, *Improving Mathematical Approaches to Geographic Profiling*, Towson, Md.: Towson University, undated. As of January 23, 2014:
http://pages.towson.edu/moleary/docs/Profiling/Report.pdf

———, "The Mathematics of Geographic Profiling," *Journal of Investigative Psychology and Offender Profiling*, Vol. 6, No. 3, October 2009, pp. 253–265.

———, "Implementing a Bayesian Approach to Criminal Geographic Profiling," *COM.Geo '10: Proceedings of the First International Conference and Exhibition on Computing for Geospatial Research and Application*, New York: Association for Computing Machinery, 2010.

———, "Modeling Criminal Distance Decay," *Cityscape*, Vol. 13, No. 3, 2011, pp. 161–198. As of January 23, 2014:
http://www.huduser.org/periodicals/cityscpe/vol13num3/Cityscape_Nov2011_Modelling_Criminal.pdf

———, "Multimodel Inference and Geographic Profiling," *Crime Mapping*, Vol. 2, No. 1, 2011.

———, "Geographic Profiling," last updated August 2012. As of January 23, 2014:
http://pages.towson.edu/moleary/profiler.html

Open Source Initiative, "The BSD 2-Clause License," undated. As of February 16, 2014:
http://opensource.org/licenses/bsd-license.php

Paulsen, Derek J., "SPIDER Crime Series Analysis Software Download Page," undated. As of January 23, 2014:
http://www.criminalbehavior.com/SPIDER

———, "Predicting Next Event Locations in a Crime Series Using Advanced Spatial Prediction Methods," briefing, United Kingdom Crime Mapping Conference, 2005. As of January 23, 2014:
http://www.ucl.ac.uk/jdi/events/mapping-conf/conf-2005/conf2005-downloads/derek-paulsen.pdf

———, "Connecting the Dots: Assessing the Accuracy of Geographic Profiling Software," *Policing*, Vol. 29, No. 2, 2006, pp. 306–334.

———, *S.P.I.D.E.R. Analysis: Using SPIDER for Tactical Crime Analysis*, edition 1.5, March 2011. As of January 23, 2014:
http://www.criminalbehavior.com/Fall2011/SPIDER%20Workbook%20and%20Powerpoint.zip

Paulsen, Derek J., Sean Bair, and Dan Helms, *Tactical Crime Analysis: Research and Investigation*, Boca Raton, Fla.: CRC Press, 2010.

Public Law 90-351, Omnibus Crime Control and Safe Streets Act of 1968, June 19, 1968.

Public Law 96-157, Justice System Improvement Act of 1979, December 27, 1979.

Ratcliffe, Jerry H., and George F. Rengert, "Near-Repeat Patterns in Philadelphia Shootings," *Security Journal*, Vol. 21, No. 1, 2008, pp. 58–76.

Rey, Sergio J., "Show Me the Code: Spatial Analysis and Open Source," *Journal of Geographical Systems*, Vol. 11, No. 2, June 2009, pp. 191–207.

Rey, Sergio J., and Luc Anselin, "PySAL: A Python Library of Spatial Analytical Methods," *Review of Regional Studies*, Vol. 37, No. 1, 2007, pp. 5–27.

———, "PySAL: A Python Library for Spatial Analytical Methods," *Handbook of Applied Spatial Analysis*, Springer-Verlag, 2010, pp. 175–193.

Rey, Sergio J., Luc Anselin, and Myunghwa Hwang, *Dynamic Manipulation of Spatial Weights Using Web Services*, unpublished manuscript, 2008.

Rich, Tom, "*School COP* Release Notes," Cambridge, Mass.: Abt Associates, September 2003.

Rich, Tom, and Peter Finn, School COP*: A Software Package for Enhancing School Safety*, Washington, D.C.: National Institute of Justice, July 2001.

———, School COP*: Implementation and Benefits in Six Sites—Final Report*, Washington, D.C.: National Institute of Justice, May 2004.

Rich, Tom, Peter Finn, and Shawn Ward, *Guide to Using* School COP *to Address Student Discipline and Crime Problems*, Washington, D.C.: U.S. Department of Justice, Office of Community Oriented Policing Services, September 20, 2001. As of January 23, 2014:
http://www.schoolcopsoftware.com/schoolcop_guide.pdf

Royce, Winston W., "Managing the Development of Large Software Systems," *Proceedings, IEEE WESCON*, Institute of Electrical and Electronics Engineers, August 1970, pp. 1–9.

School COP Software, home page, undated (a). As of January 23, 2014:
http://www.schoolcopsoftware.com

———, "*School COP*: Free Software for Supporting School-Based Problem Solving," undated (b). As of January 23, 2014:
http://www.schoolcopsoftware.com/COPS-3.html

———, "*School COP* Setup and Customization Worksheet," Cambridge, Mass.: Abt Associates, undated (c). As of January 23, 2014:
http://www.schoolcopsoftware.com/SchoolCOPSetupWorksheet.doc

———, "Instructions for Installing School COP 1.1 on a Network," September 2002a. As of January 23, 2014:
http://www.schoolcopsoftware.com/multi-user_setup.doc

———, "*School COP* Viewer Version 1.2.8," November 13, 2002b. As of January 23, 2014:
http://www.schoolcopsoftware.com/viewer_instructions.doc

Smith, Susan C., and Christopher W. Bruce, "CrimeStat III," briefing slides, undated. As of January 23, 2014:
http://www.icpsr.umich.edu/CrimeStat/workbook/CrimeStat_III_Workbook_PowerPoint.ppt

———, CrimeStat® *III User Workbook*, Washington, D.C.: National Institute of Justice, June 2008. As of January 23, 2014:
http://www.icpsr.umich.edu/CrimeStat/workbook/CrimeStat_Workbook.pdf

SourceForge, undated home page. As of January 23, 2014:
http://sourceforge.net

"SPIDER Training Day 1: Introduction and Overview," undated briefing slides.

"SPIDER Training Day 2: Using SPIDER," undated briefing slides.

"SPIDER Training Day 3: Using SPIDER Analysis," undated briefing slides.

Temple University, "Facility Cop Software," undated (a). As of January 23, 2014:
http://www.temple.edu/cj/faccop

———, "Near Repeat Calculator," undated (b). As of January 23, 2014:
http://www.temple.edu/cj/misc/nr/

———, *Facility Cop Help Manual: Prison and Jail Incident Mapping and Database Software*, Philadelphia, Pa., June 2005.

Urban Operations Research, "Urban Crime Simulator (Version 1.0)," undated. As of February 16, 2014:
http://gis.kent.edu/urbancrimesimulator/UCS_1.0/

U.S. Department of Justice, *The Department of Justice Systems Development Life Cycle Guidance Document*, Washington, D.C., January 2003. As of January 23, 2014:
http://www.justice.gov/jmd/irm/lifecycle/table.htm

U.S. Department of Justice, Office of Justice Programs, National Institute of Justice, and South Carolina Research Authority, "Geospatial Technology Working Group Meeting Minutes," Arlington, Va., October 14–15, 2010.

Whitten, Jeffrey L., Lonnie D. Bentley, and Kevin C. Dittman, *Systems Analysis and Design Methods*, 6th ed., New York: McGraw-Hill/Irwin, 2003.

Wilson, Ronald, Derek Paulsen, and Jay Lee, *Toward the Development of a Simulator for Residential Burglaries in Urban Areas: A Review of Literature on Burglary and Simulation Approaches*, 4th ed., Kent, Ohio: Kent State University, December 1, 2009.

Wong, Carolyn, "A Successful Software Development," *IEEE Transactions on Software Engineering*, Vol. 10, No. 6, November 1984, pp. 714–727.